I'M A SURVIVOR, NOT A VICTIM

THE EXPERIENCES OF NORMANDY VETERAN GEORGE CARVELL

BY

AMANDA SHEPHERD

Lammi
Publishing Inc.

Published by Lammi Publishing, Inc., headquartered in Coaldale, Alberta, Canada. http://lammipublishing.ca

Text editing by Karen Hann

Cover design by Paul Hewitt, Battlefield Design

This book is dedicated to my great-great Uncle George Carvell (1923-2009). He lived an amazingly full life and had more experiences that most could imagine. He will always be fondly remembered by all who loved him.

Contents

TABLE OF FIGURES

TIMELINE

1923—George Carvell born

5 November 1938—Carvell's father passes away

3 September 1939—Britain declares war on Germany

10 September 1939—Canada declares war on Germany

December 1939—First Canadian Infantry Division
arrives in Britain

June 1940—Fall of France

July-October 1940—Battle of Britain. Canadians protecting
Britain from a German attack

August 1940—Second Canadian Infantry Division
arrives in Britain

1941—Canadians begin large scale training exercises

December 1941—Japanese attack Hong Kong where the
Canadians are stationed

January 1942—Carvell enlists in the army

June 1942—Carvell sent to Britain

August 1942—Dieppe Raid

Early 1943—Planning begins for the Normandy Invasion
(Operation Overload)

1943—Training begins for Operation Overload

Summer 1943—First Canadian Infantry Division sent to Italy

Early 1944—Training for Operation Overload intensifies

March 1944—Carvell joins the Royal Winnipeg Rifles

6 June 1944—Normandy Invasion landings

8 June 1944—Battle of Putot-en-Bessin

8 June 1944—Carvell captured

6 May 1945—Carvell liberated

8 May 1945—Germany surrenders

INTRODUCTION

This project has been adapted from my Masters' thesis, an academic examination of my great-great uncle George Carvell's time during the Second World War and his experiences as a prisoner of war (POW), set within the larger context of Canada's role in the conflict, particularly the reinforcement units and the POWs.

During my oral thesis examination, one of the examiners asked me, "Why is this story important? Why is it worthy of a thesis?" My first thoughts when asked that question was that it was obvious that this was worthy of a thesis, but I quickly realized that I needed to justify why I believed it. The main reason I gave was it was more than just a story about my great-great uncle. It was an examination of one man's experience set in the larger role of Canada in the war. The thesis examined aspects of the Canadian war experience that often is glossed over, or little has been written about the reinforcement units, Battle of Putot-en-Bessin, and Normandy POWs. The scope of research made it more than just a 'soldier biography' that high school students write. It made it a master's thesis.

On a personal level, George Carvell's story, is to me, that of my great-great uncle, a man loved and respected by his family and community, a man I personally admired very much. However, his story also belongs within the larger context of the Canadian Second World War narrative because he was there.

Simple as it sounds, he was there.

George Carvell, eldest son of a family of seven, was there, endlessly training with the reinforcement units in the fields of Britain, taking fire on the blood-soaked beaches of Normandy, fighting to take back the village of Putot-en-Bessin from the Germans, and labouring under harsh conditions in the POW camps for meager rations. This time is slipping away from living memory... only a fraction of those who saw firsthand are alive to tell their tales.

Thus, it is up to us, the younger generation, to do everything we can to preserve their stories. During one of the D-Day ceremonies held for the 70th Anniversary that I attended in France, two French teens spoke that it was our responsibility, the next generation, to take the torch of remembrance from these men and women so their stories would not be forgotten. We must listen to the recollections of the few who are still with us. For those who are not, we must (as I have), comb the records and piece together the tales from the fragments of information that we can find. My great-great uncle spoke little of his wartime experiences during his life. It has only been after his death that I have been able to see his full service record and gather enough pieces to construct the narrative of his time overseas.

Though this story is intensely personal to myself and my family, I, as a history scholar, am well aware that George Carvell's story does not exist within a vacuum. It is part of a larger narrative, a larger truth, about the lives and experiences of the thousands of Canadian farm boys, timber men, labourers, mechanics, teachers, fishermen, and those of countless other occupations who lay down their shovels, saws, hammers, wrenches, chalk, and nets to take up arms and defend the lives of people they'd never met.

What follows in this narrative is the story I was able to find. Yes, it is the story of my great-great uncle, the timber man who took up arms, but it is also part of the story of Canada, the war we fought, and the profound way it changed us as a nation.

CHAPTER ONE

A NATION GOES TO WAR

August 14, 1914, the British futurist author H. G. Wells published the first of a series of articles in *the Daily News* entitled "The War that will End War." The phrase became popular in its alternate form as 'the war to end all wars.' Four years and seventeen million deaths later, the Great War, eventually called the First World War, was over. History has shown the tragic irony of Wells's prediction. It would be less than twenty-one years of peace before the Second World War broke out. This conflict spanned six years and cost over sixty million lives.

An ocean away from the battlefields, Canada quickly joined the Allied fight alongside the British and French and pledging the lives of another generation of Canadians to witness the horrors of war. Even with the Great War fresh in the minds of the nation, 58,000 joined to fight Germany in 1939. One of these men was George Carvell, a 19-year-old timber man from Plaster Rock, New Brunswick. He was a son, a brother, a friend, and a proud Canadian.

For George Carvell and thousands of others, a sense of duty was the deciding factor in joining the military. His life would change dramatically from this choice. He would go from the timber mills of New Brunswick to the training fields of Britain, the beaches of Normandy, the battlefield of Putot-en-Bessin, a narrow and horrifying escape from death at the Chateau d'Audrieux, a series of POW and concentration camps, back to Britain, and finally back home. While his combat activities were brief, his experience as a prisoner of war shaped the rest of his life.

It would be impossible to properly tell my great-great uncle's story without the stories of so many of these other men, both on a micro and a macro scale. I must tell the story of the war itself. I must tell the story of the training camps. I must tell the story of the battles that led to his time as a POW. I must tell the horrifying tale of how he almost came to be among the numbers murdered by the 12th SS Panzer Division (Hitler Youth). I must tell the story of the POW and concentration camps, how they could test the extremes of man's inhumanity to man, and how this affected the survivors. I must also tell of my great-great uncle's resilience, and how he used his experiences to bring about awareness of the horrors of war and the need for remembrance to the next generations.

The images of the Great War were still on the minds of Canadians when they were met with another war in 1939. Most Canadians could not imagine leaving the British to fight another major conflict alone; however, the country was deeply divided on how to help Britain after the Great War. Prime Minister William Lyon Mackenzie King was well aware of the divide that the Great War had produced and did not want to see that occur again. King decided that Canada would plan for a modest war effort of supplies and food, and not send another generation to slaughter.[1] Initially, Canada's primary contribution to the war effort was its navy, a few Royal Canadian Air Force squadrons, and Canadians flying in the British Royal Air Force. Ground divisions needed time to be trained before they could be sent overseas.

Once the Canadian Army was in Britain in late 1939, they expected to only stay in Britain for a few weeks or months before seeing battle. The men believed that they would fight with the British regiments as they did in the Great War. However, the fall of France in 1940 drastically changed the role the Canadians would play. The Canadians were now in charge of the defence of Britain. Training was constant, and it often simulated a German attack on the country. Large scaled exercises served the purpose of evaluating what the soldiers had learned and what areas needed more focus. Training occurred at the individual level to the divisional level, with all the troops involved. The constant training, without real battles, left many of the men discouraged and questioning why they had enlisted. Many men got into trouble during this time because of the boredom. The Canadians overseas did not see battle until August 19, 1942, when the 2nd Canadian Infantry Division led the Dieppe Raid. The failure of the raid and the immense loss of lives changed how the men approached their training.

Planning began in 1943 for a cross-Channel attack into France that would take place in 1944 in the Normandy region of northern France. This battle is often referred to as the Normandy campaign or D-Day. The code name given to the attack the planners was Operation Overlord. Every military operation has a different code name, used so that the enemy does not know any details that could give away locations or important information. This invasion would be a joint effort from the Americans, Canadians and Britons. The Canadians played an important role in this invasion and with the liberation of Europe from the Nazis.

Like most Canadian soldiers, George Carvell participated in numerous training courses. He was transferred to the Royal Winnipeg Rifles (RWR), part of 7th Canadian Infantry Brigade, before the Normandy invasion and participated in it. Surviving the initial assault was a miracle when so many others lost their lives, including one of his friends, William Smith. The Winnipegs lost over 130 members on D-Day alone.[2] The literature on the Normandy invasion is vast, and scholars have made significant arguments about Canada's role and whether it was a success or failure. The subsequent battles after the initial beach landings led to even more Canadian casualties and more controversy.

The Royal Winnipeg Rifles, George Carvell among them, battled fiercely against the Germans at Putot-en-Bessin. Putot-en-Bessin was a small village in northern France by the Caen-Bayeux rail line. It had houses and farms built out of Caen stone, making each a potential stronghold. Wheat field surrounding the village obscured the battlefield and left the Winnipegs little lines of sight. Some historians believe that the Canadians should have been able to hold this town, and its loss on 8 June 1944 revealed the lack of training the soldiers had.[3] It can be easy to see how some historians would blame the soldiers for the poor showing at Putot by just looking at the maps of the area. Once you set foot on the grounds, which I was able to do during my study tour, it is easy to see how difficult a place it would be to defend with poor sight lines and no real stronghold places the soldiers could hold. Recent scholarship has contested this claim and contends that the defence of Putot and the Regina Rifles at Brettville as a great Canadian achievement. Carvell was taken prisoner at Putot-en-Bessin, along with 140 of his fellow soldiers, beginning a new phase of his war experience that was filled with pain, illness, biting physical labour, uncertainty, and a new and horrifying comprehension of the extent of man's inhumanity to man. Unlike many others, it concluded with a joyful release and homecoming.

CHAPTER TWO

A BOY, AND THEN A TIMBER MAN

George Carvell was born on 15 August, 1923, in Saint John, New Brunswick to William and Emma Carvell, the fourth out of seven children and the eldest son. He had five sisters (three older: Thelma, Ruth, and Pearl, and two younger: Verna Dea and Christina) and one younger brother, Roy. The tight-knit family was raised in Saint John. However, when George was ten years old, his parents moved the family to Plaster Rock, a small village in northern New Brunswick, while his father was out of work. The main sources for work there were farming and the lumber mills. The family only stayed in Plaster Rock for a short period before moving back to Saint John when their father went back to work. Growing up, Carvell enjoyed fishing, hunting, and any outdoor activities. Softball was one of his favorite sports.

Carvell completed grade five before starting in the work-force at the age of twelve. He was considered to be fairly intelligent and eager to learn. When his father passed away on 5 November 1938, he believed that it was his duty to help support his mother and siblings, being the eldest male of the family. The family moved back to Plaster Rock after William's passing, where it was easier to find steady work. George's sister Pearl married Otis Kierstead in September 1937. The family continued growing when Pearl and Otis had their only daughter, Arlene— my grandmother—in 1940.

The Maritimes were hit hard during the Depression; it was the hardest-hit region east of the Prairies. The Maritimes were no stranger to hard economic times, due to their economy being dependent on primary production and international trade. However, this depression was more severe due to the lack of federal government help, and the borders were closed for emigration. One of the main obstacles that the citizens of the Maritimes faced was the lack of government relief. The municipalities were responsible for that, but most of the smaller municipalities of New Brunswick did not have the revenue to make the government relief programs work.[4] Unemployment was high among woods and mill workers. Even with the struggles the province was experiencing, young George Carvell was able to continue working. He worked as a farm labourer for a few years doing various jobs around farms in Victoria County. He began working as a timber man in May 1940 at a mill in Plaster Rock.[5] His duties included cutting, trimming and piling wood. He also worked as an axeman teamster and on a saw crew. Carvell stayed at this job until he enlisted in the military.

George Carvell was very close with both his immediate and large extended family. He was always known to me as Uncle George. He was my great-great uncle, my great grandmother's brother, and the uncle who made me my duck bank when I was little. When I was a child, my mother, brother and I would go every summer up to visit him and Uncle Roy in Plaster Rock. It was always easy to pick out Uncle George's house because of the large sunflowers that grew all around his property. He was always willing to spend time with his family. It was evident how important family was to him; even as he was getting older, he would always ask how the great-great nieces and nephews were even if he could not always remember our names. He would always want the family to visit with him when he was in the hospital for his cancer treatments and the family was always happy to visit.

Carvell was five feet six inches and a hundred and fifty pounds at his enlistment. He had brown eyes and dark brown hair; however, I only ever knew his head to be bald. Both George and his younger brother Roy had dark complexions compared to their sisters, who were fair. He had a strong upper body from all his years working at the mill and time spent outside. If you had met George, you would have noticed that he was not a large man in stature but that did not stop him from having a larger-than-life personality. He had a presence about him that you noticed as soon as he walked into the room. George's boisterousness could sometimes scare children, which often happened with my mother and my aunts when they were young. My mother would often tell me stories about how Uncle George would chase her around the house just to scare and tease her. The family has suggested that the reason he had such a loud personality was from his experiences in the war and a need to ensure that he would not be a forgotten man, as many POWs felt they were.

George had a great sense of humour and loved to tease, tell jokes, and play pranks on people, especially children. He was also a man who did not hesitate to express his strong opinions, including his dislike for turnips and his refusal to eat fiddleheads because even deer would not eat them. George loved to be outside and enjoyed his time hunting, four-wheeling, and gardening. He also loved to play card games with anyone who was willing to play. Any time he played cribbage, he would boast that no one would be able to beat him. When I would make the attempt to play cribbage with him, it always ended with him winning. He could count the cards before I even had a chance to look at them. George would spend a lot of time teasing you while playing the game especially boasting that he was going to "skunk" you and you would be really lucky if he didn't double "skunk" you. He spent much of his spare time making woodwork for his family and friends. Their houses were filled with ornament shelves, nightstands, and duck banks for the children. I am lucky to have three pieces of woodwork in my house all made from Uncle George.

While family was important to Carvell, his community was also very important. He was always an active member especially when it came to remembering the war. He participated in numerous Remembrance Day ceremonies and projects. In 2007, he began going into the local elementary school and speaking to the students about his experiences and being a good citizen. At the school, he and another veteran worked with a teacher who believed that remembrance was vital for the next generation to learn. He continued with these school visits until he passed away in 2009. George was also an active member of the Royal Canadian Legion Marble Arch Branch #29 for 65 years. The love the community had for him was evident at his funeral in 2009. Many of the students to whom he spoke at the school even came to pay their last respects to him. He lived a long, full life. The family and the community mourned for the loss of such a great man but celebrated that they knew George.

The family always knew that Uncle George had served in Normandy during the war and had spent eleven months as a POW. He never liked to talk about his experiences. When asked, he would always reply "that it was something I had to do" and that he would do it again if needed. He never provided a reason as to why he did not want to tell his family the details of his experiences. Was he trying to save his family from living with his suffering, or was he just not able to put the experiences into words? George was the only person who could answer that question. We knew that his strong dislike of turnips came from his experiences in the POW camps. They were often served turnip soup as the only food. We also knew that he believed that he was treated as well as could be under the circumstances, and he would go to war again if the need arose.

CHAPTER THREE

FILLING IN THE BLANKS

From childhood onward, I'd always been fascinated by Uncle George's war story. It was exciting to know that I had a relative who'd landed on Juno Beach and survived being a prisoner of war. There were not many of my friends who could say the same. My interest grew more when my grandmother gave me a letter that he wrote to my great-grandmother, Pearl, during his time in Britain. Each time that I saw Uncle George after that, I wanted to ask him about his experience. However, the family told me that Uncle George did not talk about what happened in the war, and he probably would not answer my questions.

My dilemma became how to ask my elderly uncle about his time in the war when he never spoke about it. Unfortunately, I did not get the chance before he passed away. When Uncle George died in 2009, I spoke to his daughter, Sandra, at the funeral about his war records and other information that she had. She told me that she would send my mother some samples of the records she had, which she did. However, it was not until a few years later that I was able to take real steps forward to fully understanding his story.

In 2013, I decided to go back to university and get my master's degree. It was Uncle George's unknown story that drew me back to school. I was accepting into the Master of Arts program through the University of New Brunswick. Originally, I wanted to link Uncle George's story with my brother's experiences in the Afghanistan War; however, the history committee told me that the topic was too big for a master's thesis and that I needed to narrow down my focus. Shortly after starting the program, I received a large brown envelope, from Sandra, containing the service record of Uncle George, the letters home from Europe, and newspapers articles that featured him years after the war. I was excited to get all of this information and see what more I could find out about his story. I quickly realized that I could not read most of what was written in the service file because I did not know how to read the military codes.

I came to understand that the image I had of my great-great uncle (though loving and respectful) was far from comprehensive. I had a meeting with my thesis supervisor to discuss the service file. Dr. Marc Milner started looking through the file and noticed one key date: 8 June, 1944. That was the day Uncle George was captured. He looked at the date and then to me and asked if I knew what this date meant, especially for the Royal Winnipeg Rifles. At this point, I had to admit that I had no idea of the significance. Dr. Milner told me that 8 June, 1944, was significant to the Winnipegs because that was the date that the 12th SS Panzer Division (Hitler Youth) murdered members of the regiment. I sat in silence as I processed what he told me. It had been pure luck that Uncle George was not murdered that day. That was profound to find out how close he was to death before his story even started.

After my initial meeting with Dr. Milner, I took some time to go through the files before going to see Dr. Lee Windsor and getting his opinion on the records. After an intense meeting with Dr. Windsor, I had a much clearer picture on what Uncle George did and the gaps that I needed to fill. We saw a story emerge of a young soldier's through training, battle, capture, and post-war life. There were many questions that needed to be answered as to why a young man from rural New Brunswick decided to join up, as well as his experiences in Britain before he'd gone into battle during the Normandy invasion. His time as a POW brought about the most questions and would also pose the most challenging aspect of his story. The challenge would be that very little secondary sources were available. The Second World War Canadian POW narrative focused on the accounts from Dieppe and Hong Kong. The literature on this topic is slim, however, for the Normandy POWs. Postcards from his time in the camps revealed very little of what the camps were like and what he was going through. Using accounts from other soldiers, I was able to obtain a more complete picture of his experiences in the first and last camp.

The family knew next to nothing of what he saw and experienced, knowing only that he believed it had been his duty to go to war, that he participated in the Normandy invasion, and that from his time as a POW he had a strong dislike for turnips. Through his service files, postcards, letters, and newspaper articles, I was able to track some of his locations during the course of his training in Britain, combat activities in Normandy and Putot-en-Bessin, and the POW camps. One of the issues that arose with the service file was that it gave little information on his activities once he went into battle and was captured. Also, because he transferred into the Royal Winnipeg Rifles in 1944, there were numerous occasions in the paperwork that stated he was with the North Shore (NB) Regiment instead of the Winnipegs. He had never been attached to the North Shore Regiment because he enlisted with the No. 7 Depot District, and he was supposed to be with the Charlton and York Regiment, but was transferred to the reinforcement units, which raises questions as to why the paperwork would stated he was in that regiment.

I knew from the information that I had in the service file, letters, and newspaper articles that an amazing story waited to be found. Just from this information, I learned details that I never knew about Uncle George's time in the service, including his training and locations he as stationed. A 1994 newspaper article featured an interview from Uncle George after his return from visiting Britain, France, and the Netherlands for the 50th anniversary of D-Day. That article added more details to this picture I was starting to paint. The next step would be to go to Ottawa to see what I could find in the archives about his time in England and the war diaries of his regiment. Both Dr. Milner and Dr. Windsor strongly suggested that I try to get on one of the Canadian battlefield study tours that would be coming up the following year. I applied to the Canadian Battlefields Foundation study tour and was accepted to go on that trip. I was excited for the opportunity to go to the different battle sites from the First and Second World Wars. What was more exciting was that I would at Juno Beach for the 70th anniversary of D-Day. I knew how special but difficult that day would be. This trip would add more information that I could add to this project and another way that I could honour Uncle George's memory.

To paint a genuine picture of my great-great uncle's experience overseas, I needed to go far beyond my own family history and my great-great uncle's service record. Uncle George did not exist in isolation. I sought out and examined numerous pieces of existing literature so I could properly place his story.

Though I sought to tell the tale of Rifleman George Carvell, I understood that his story was a chapter in the overall narrative of Canada in the Second World War, our nation's place within the battles and the politics. As a writer and a scholar, I was fortunate to be able to learn from and borrow from the work of those who have examined this subject before me. The body of literature on the Normandy campaign is vast, including numerous documents about training for the operation and the invasion. I needed to examine that first. Beyond that, I had to look at what has already been written about POWs so that I might give Carvell's story that context.

I quickly discovered that the body of Canadian literature on the prisoner of war experience is modest. The stories of prisoners of war in Hong Kong and Dieppe are the most well-known. There exists little information about the prisoners of war that were captured in Normandy. Most of what is written covers the murders of Canadian prisoners of war by the 12th SS Panzer Division (Hitler Youth), the incident that had first sparked my advisor's attention to the narrative. But I knew that my great-great uncle's story extended far beyond those events.

Training the Canadian Army for this campaign took place over a four-year period while troops were stationed in Britain. Carvell was in the 1st Canadian Reinforcement Unit for a year before moving to the 7th Infantry Reinforcement Unit. To understand how training may have contributed to issues at

Normandy, I looked at John A. English's *The Canadian Army and the Normandy Campaign: A Study of Failure of High Command* (1991). The book makes no mention of the training of the reinforcement units.

As I examined the records and coverage that did exist, I found myself asking many questions. What training did the units receive? What did the reinforcement units do when the regular regiments were involved in the large-scale exercises? Did the regular regimental officers drop in to the reinforcement units to direct them in the newest training so these units would be in sync with all the others?

I found some answers in Colonel C.P. Stacey's *Six Years of War—The Army in Canada, Britain, and the Pacific* (1955), but he only glosses over the training the reinforcement units received which left me looking elsewhere for more information.

Two articles in the 2006 *Canadian Military History* journal gave me a bit of a breakthrough. They detail the letters of Captain Harold MacDonald to his wife while he was overseas during the war, describing life for a Canadian soldier in Britain, from the leaves to London, the letter/parcels from home, to the training courses that he took.

Though these texts were indeed essential for my under-standing of Normandy, I found them at the same time disheartening because they were so critical of the Canadian Army's performance there. I felt that the texts had ignored key factors (along with the reinforcement units). I was relieved to come across the work of Terry Copp, who changed the Normandy paradigm when he published his ground-breaking work *Fields of Fire: The Canadians in Normandy* (2003). Copp disagrees with Stacey's assessment that the Canadians had a lackluster showing and the Germans were a superior fighting force.

As I read, the picture began to form more clearly, gathering depth and perspective as I sought to understand what Uncle George and the Canadians faced during the Normandy invasion and the days that followed.

The Normandy invasion was just another battle in the long history of the Royal Winnipeg Rifles. Brian A. Reid's *Named by the Enemy: A History of the Royal Winnipeg Rifles* (2010) adds firsthand accounts and published sources to the war diaries. Uncle's George's experiences could easily fit within this regimental history, especially after he joined the regiment before D-Day and his capture on 8 June, 1944. I found an account of letters written by two brothers to be particularly striking. They described their fears in letters to their mother before going into this battle, having been told that they would not make it home again.[6] This further illustrated to me the realities that the Canadian soldiers had to endure before and after the invasion.

While Reid uses firsthand accounts to add in the personal connection to the Winnipeg's official history, Jean Portugal's series *We Were There* (1998) contains only firsthand accounts from the soldiers of the Second World War. In Volume 6, Portugal focuses on the Winnipegs and their participation in the Normandy invasion, the battle of Putot-en-Bessin, and the liberation of Europe. The detailed accounts from their soldiers provide the human connection that is often left out or minimized in the literature (which is one reason why I wrote this book). These accounts were, however, given many years after the war. Memories can change and fade over time; still, these accounts were important. Some moments, particularly the Normandy landings and the battle of Putot-en-Bessin, must have remained vividly in the minds of these men. Many described these experiences in detail even years after the fact. Though he never spoke of it, the memories likely also remained in the mind of my great-great uncle.

Though I was finding some good information, a constant frustration remained the lack of information about the Normandy POWs from the Canadian Forces. The majority of Canadian POW research is on the Dieppe prisoners and those captured in Hong Kong by the Japanese. Those men had different experiences in captivity. Daniel Dancocks's *In Enemy Hands* (1983) is a popular history[7]; however, it still is a useful beginning for studying the subject of Canadian POWs, as it provides firsthand accounts from members of the army, air force, and navy who were all captured during different periods of the war. Dancocks argues that Canadian prisoners of war are the forgotten men of World War II.[8] Reading that just galvanized me further; I would not allow Uncle George to be forgotten.

One of the more disturbing details of Uncle George's time as a POW is how easily he could have ended up a subject of Howard Margolian's *Conduct Unbecoming: The Story of the Murder of Canadian Prisoners of War in* Normandy (1998). Margolian states that he wrote the book for two reasons. The first was a warning of what can happen when soldiers are dehumanized by political indoctrination, the encouragement of ugly prejudices, and the creed of blind obedience. The second purpose is to honour oft-forgotten and occasionally scorned heroes.[9]

One of my more exciting research finds was a book by Will R. Bird entitled *Two Jacks: The Amazing Adventures of Major Jack M. Veness and Major Jack L. Fairweather* (1955). Veness and Fairweather, of the North Novas, were captured during the Battle of Authie on 7 June 1944 and marched to the Abbeye d'Ardenne before being moved to a POW camp.[10] They ended up at the Rennes prison camp, the same as my great-great uncle. This book was a gold mine, filling in many of the blanks of Uncle George's first camp experience, which he was unable to describe the camp in his letter home.[11]

If I was going to be thorough about presenting my great-great uncle's story, I couldn't simply look just at the Normandy POWs. I also needed to understand the experiences of the Canadian soldiers in the Japanese POW camps. The Normandy POW experience was vastly different from those captured at Hong Kong by the Japanese. Charles G Roland's book *Long Night's Journey into Night: Prisoners of War in Hong Kong and Japan, 1941-1945* (2001) describes the treatment and means of survival that the men found.

I was fortunate to find more useful information in Jonathan Vance's *Objects of Concern: Canadian Prisoners of War Through the Twentieth Century* (1994). The text examines the treatment of POWs through both world wars, the effort made at home, and the reintegration of ex-POWs into society. As George Carvell did indeed need to integrate back into society, I was glad to read the accounts of others who had done the same.

Jack A Poolton's memoir *Destined to Survive: A Dieppe Veteran's Story* (1998) describes his battle and captivity experiences after that disastrous Canadian defeat. Dieppe prisoners did not have to endure as much brutality as their Hong Kong counterparts, but this does not mean that their POW stays were easy. Part of the problem was that Canadian troops had never been taught how to handle such a capture. One significant statement that Poolton writes about his capture was, "you can train a soldier to fight and you can train a soldier to accept death, but there is no way to prepare a soldier to be taken prisoner."[12] This is a common theme among POWs, especially those captured at Dieppe. Uncle George never received training on what to do if he was captured during his training in Britain. It was no until after the Normandy invasion that the Canadian Army started giving the men training on the possibility being captured and what they could do. Unfortunately, it was too late for Uncle George.

The memoires of another Dieppe prisoner, A. Robert Prouse, entitled *Ticket to Hell via Dieppe* (1982) describes his experiences in the POW hospital and camps, as well as his escape attempts. Treatment changed depending on the camp the men were in. Some camps were overcrowded and unable to handle their populations. What I found striking about this text was how, even with the lack of food, lack of space, and long work days, the Dieppe POWs were still able to find ways to keep morale lifted and make the best of the situation. I suspect that my optimistic Uncle George had done much of the same.

Upon coming home, George Carvell faced the scourge of countless soldiers: battle exhaustion. It's the same condition that was known as shell shock in the First World War, and it is now known as Post-Traumatic Stress Disorder (PTSD). Terry Copp and Bill McAndrew's book *Battle Exhaustion: Soldiers and Psychiatrics in the Canadian Army, 1939-1945* (1990) examines battle exhaustion through the war and measures that were used to combat this problem.

With the literature on the Normandy invasion so vast, I had to question whether my great-great uncle's story could bring anything new to the discussion. What made his story worthy of remembrance? What made it special. His story is not special just because he is family; his story sets to fill in some of the holes that are missing from the canon. The training with the reinforcement units are mostly left out from the literature. Discussing the regimental war diaries and personal accounts of Carvell and others will help establish a better understanding of the training. His time spent as a POW is just as significant as his time in Britain training. The fact that he was able to survive the eleven months in numerous camps and marches was a miracle. This part of his story is largely unknown to most Canadians, and writing his story gave me the chance to share it.

CHAPTER FOUR

BECOMING SOLDIERS: THE CANADIAN ARMY IN CANADA AND BRITAIN

The Second World War changed the lives of most Canadians. Thousands flocked to join the military and were sent to Britain. George Carvell was one of that number. He enlisted out of a sense of duty. His father had passed away, and being the eldest male in the family, he felt that it was his place. Carvell was working to support his family. The family was dealing with hard times since the Depression struck and he thought enlisting would be the best way to support them.

Training for battle was the main priority of the Canadian army during the years spent in garrison in Britain. There has been considerable criticism, from historians C. P. Stacey and John English, of the training the Canadians obtained. The reinforcement units were an important part of the army. Many men coming into the reinforcement units from Canada had gone through basic, but required more advanced training before moving to a regiment. Operation Overlord changed the focus on training for all units that would be involved. The focus shifted from protecting Britain to assaulting a beachhead. However, questions have arisen due to the Canadians' showing during that battle. Stacey believed the Canadians did not achieve everything they should have after all the time they'd had to develop their skills. He believed that they used brute force rather than tactics and strategy to win the ground. Training in Britain was a vital part of the soldier's life there, but many enjoyed time in the cities with British families and women. A quarter of a million Canadians called Britain home during the war, and that transformed not only the Canadians but also the British who took these soldiers in as their own.

Britain officially declared war on 3 September 1939, after Germany invaded Poland. Canada did not declare war on Germany until 10 September, a week later. The Canadian government had already decided to give Britain their full support before officially declaring war. Prime Minister William Lyon Mackenzie King believed in the British Empire; however, he believed that Canada could not endure another slaughter like the Great War. He also wanted to avoid another divisive debate over conscription such as the one that occurred in 1917.[13] He planned for a modest war effort, mostly being a supplier of munitions and food for the British. While King wanted to limit the Canadian war effort to only supplies, others in the government believed that Canada needed to send troops to the aid of Britain. Hitler threatened more than just Europe, and Canada needed to stand up and defend.

The public reaction to this declaration of war was substantially different from the First World War. There was a sizable faction of Canadians who wanted nothing to do with another war among European states. They did not relish in the thought of being thrown into harm's way as they had been during the Great War. In his memoirs, Lieutenant General Howard Graham described, the country's overall reaction to the war, saying: "there was little enthusiasm for the war in 1939 and 'the cause' that had been present in 1914."[14] No Canadians stood in the streets and cheered the end of the twenty-year armistice when Canada went to war with Nazi Germany. Howard did not want to go back to war; he had a family and a career. However, he knew it was his duty to fight, because his regiment was mobilizing. Howard's thoughts on going to war again were not unique; even still, thousands of men quickly volunteered. Some men did not want to go to war at all and waited until they were conscripted. Tom Didmon had no interest in battle. He wanted to stay in Canada and work on the home front. He was conscripted.[15] I read Didmon's memoir about his experiences during the war while researching Carvell's story, and it was different than most.

The volunteers had different reasons for wanting to enlist. Howard spoke of duty, which was one of the main reasons. Other reasons that men spoke of were patriotism, a quest for adventure, a desire to escape the boredom of everyday life, and the need to fight the Nazis before they overwhelmed the world.[16] Some drifted into the service, inspired by a speech, urged on by mates, or fortified by drink. The Great Depression had also left thousands of men without jobs, and many young men had never had a job until they enlisted. Steady work, food, and money for their families was enough incentive to join. While the Depression did push some into the service, of those who enlisted within the first three months, 89 percent left jobs.[17]

The requirements for men to enlist were established in 1938. Men who were accepted into the military would be placed in either the category for which they were fit within general service or employed in their specialized trades or lines of communication.[18] Men had to be between eighteen and forty-five years old. Underage soldiers were told to come back when they were of age; however, many forged their documents and lied to get in. Initially, the rate of rejection for medical ailments was high, and something as simple as rotting teeth kept many men from the army.[19] Chest measurements had to be at least 34 inches. The minimum height was five feet four inches, but for the horse and field artillerymen it was five feet six. Gunners needed to be at least five feet seven inches.[20] Originally, men had to be British subjects and of good character; however, by the end of 1939 this requirement was dropped. Overworked medical boards did not take the time to carefully evaluate all recruits, and many men with history of mental illness and mental deficiencies were enrolled in the army.[21]

By 1940, the general physical requirements for recruits dropped. Stacey surmises that this was to increase numbers of accepted men. Medical boards were also given new instructions in early 1940. Doctors had to establish if the recruit was sufficiently intelligent by questioning him. The doctors were also told that the obvious men who could not enlist would be defined as those with a history of nervous breakdowns, residence in an institution, drug additions, or a family history indicating nervous instability such as migraines or eccentricity.[22] The hope was to avoid the amount of shell shock cases that had occurred during the Great War.

By the end of September, 58,337 men had enlisted, including over 4,000 veterans from the First World War. Many of the veterans who saw conflict in the First World War were average or medically unfit.[23] Most of the volunteers were very young. Two-thirds of the volunteers were between the ages of eighteen and twenty-five, and there was a great divide between the officers and men with formal education. Most of the ranks had ended their education with the seventh grade.[24]

CHAPTER FIVE

THE TIMBER MAN ENLISTS: CANADA AND THE TRAINING OF A CITIZEN ARMY

Figure 1: Carvell's enlistment photo, 1942.
Author's personal collection.

George Carvell finally enlisted on 5 January 1942, a few months after his nineteenth birthday. He tried to enlist earlier than 1942; however, when he went to the local recruitment office, he was turned down because someone at the office knew him and knew he was too young. When he did finally manage to successfully enlist, he joined the No. 7 District Depot in Fredericton, New Brunswick.

The Carvells were a close family and made sure that they were all in attendance (except Pearl who was in Saint John) when he left for his basic training in Edmundston. In the pictures of the day, the family smiled but no one knew what the future held. None of them imagined that in just over two years, they would not know if their brother was dead or alive.

Figure 2: Carvell (back row, second to the right) with him friends who enlisted with him.

Figure 3: Carvell with his sister's Ruth (left) and Thelma (right). Author's personal collection.

Home and overseas training of the Canadian military evolved throughout the war. Initial training began in Canada shortly after enlistment. Each province had their own basic training facilities, and New Brunswick had numerous camps to provide the soldiers with basic marching and military drills.

Carvell was sent to the No. 71 Canadian Army (basic) Training Centre Edmundston on 5 February 1942 and was attached to this unit until being sent overseas. The centre first opened in 1940 and it was changed into a basic training facility in 1941. Carvell received the basic training in drill, physical training, first aid, marching, small arms training, gas training, fieldcraft, and map reading. Initial training normally would last eight weeks unless circumstances dictated otherwise. Carvell trained there until April 1942, when he was sent to Aldershot, Nova Scotia to continue.

Aldershot was the site of advanced infantry training during the First World War and the army used it again for the Second World War training.[25] Soldiers went there after they had completed their basic training. This area was chosen because of the larger terrain, which allowed more realistic training for larger groups and classes. Advanced training lasted up to nine weeks. They engaged in such learning activities as physical training, marching, bayonet fighting, judging distance, digging and wiring, field training and sub-machine gun.[26] They also received training on different weapons. After his initial training, Carvell was described by his lieutenant as being "not particularly ambitious, but liked army life very well. He seemed rather quiet and dependable, probably able to enjoy himself and take care of himself."[27] Carvell stayed at Aldershot until he was sent to Britain on 2 June 1942, where he would join the Carleton and York Regiment.

Chapter Six

Training Steps Up in Britain

When Carvell arrived in Britain on 11 June 1942, the Canadians had been training there for almost two and a half years. They had set up the training centres in Aldershot, Britain, which was thirty miles southwest of London, and others around southern Britain. The first set of Canadian soldiers to arrive in Aldershot came on 17 December 1939. These were raw recruits who required individual training, and they made up more than half of the 1st Canadian Infantry Division.[28] None of the soldiers who first arrived in Britain believed that they would be staying there for more than a few weeks or months at the most before they went into battle. The fall of France in June 1940 changed all of that. During those initial years, training evolved into three main phases. The first phase was from 1939—40, when the 1st Canadian Division and the ancillary troops were trained with a view to join the British Expeditionary Force in France. The second phase consisted of training to fit the units for the defence of Britain. The third phase of training was for offensive operations abroad.[29]

For the men and their units, there were two stages of the initial training: individual and collective. The individual training was designed to teach the soldiers discipline and the handling of their weapons and equipment. Collective training was designed so the soldiers would learn to work as part of a team in tactical manoeuvres.[30] When the Canadian Army first arrived in Britain, the troops had only the most elementary of training. Therefore, Major-General A. G. L. McNaughton set about training his men. He followed an unrelenting succession of physical training, anti-gas and small-arms drill, lectures, route marches, and mock battles to test battle skills, in a drive to make the men fit enough to face the hardened German Army.[31] The days were long, starting at 0800 hours and ending at 2000 hours, Monday to Friday. Saturdays, men received a small reprieve on training, finishing at 1600 hours.[32] Sundays were generally free days for the men, with church services provided in the mornings. The Canadians needed to train hard before they could face the German Army. The Germans had started re-arming in 1935, and thousands of men had enlisted. They started training immediately; therefore, had almost five years of extra training and thousands more soldiers than the Canadians did.

With the fall of France in June 1940, the training shifted from joining the British Expeditionary Force to defending Britain. The Canadians would spend the next two and a half years preparing for this specific task. It was also during this period that the Canadians moved to the Northamptonshire to await the expected invasion from the Germans. Brigade-level training began, but there was no opportunity yet for divisional exercises.[33] The brigades needed to train together to understand what was required of the men when fighting together. Emphasis was placed on brigade and battalion groups participating in rapid movements by motor transport and units practiced night moves. Rapid movements included moving the units on short notice as quickly and as in an organized manner as possible without confusion. Night moves had the soldiers move in their units after dark. The soldiers needed to be able to move as a unit to defend properly.

Even with this new emphasis on brigade-level training, the commanders quickly realized that individual training was necessary. Soldiers did not enjoy it; however, they knew that it had to be done. The 2nd Canadian Division, which began arriving in Britain in the summer of 1940, lagged in the individual training of their soldiers. The Division focused in, and by Christmas of 1940, they were sufficiently prepared for active duty. Even with equipment shortages, the Canadians continued to train at all levels.

Large scale exercises began in 1941. Throughout 1941 and the early part of 1942, all the major exercises had an anti-invasion theme. Exercises Fox (February) and Dog (March) were intended to practice the 1st and 2nd Divisions respectively, in a move by road transport to concentration area, an advance to contact with a hostile force, and the issuing of orders for deployment and attack.[34] Stacey argues that these exercises showed that neither division was very efficient in acting as a formed body and that they needed to train further to achieve the necessary strength and skill. The traffic control problem of the Exercises Fox and Dog received close attention.[35] There were significant traffic jams, and the artillery could not get forward to support infantry attacks.

Exercise Waterloo (June 1941) was the first exercise in which the Canadian Corps as a whole took part. This exercise involved about half the soldiers in Britain. The main objective was for the Canadians to practice being in a counter attack role. They were able to develop an attack against the enemy position and drive the invaders back to the sea.[36] The divisions had a better showing during this exercise than the previous two. The largest exercise so far staged in Britain was Bumper (September). It consisted of two army headquarters, four corps, and twelve divisions. As with the other exercises, this kept with the anti-invasion theme. Stacey describes the main criticism of this exercise was the positions of the headquarters, which were too far back, the failure to pass information, and the continued use of the brigade-group system of handling divisions.[37] Each of these exercises helped the command learn where they needed to focus on for training and to become stronger divisions. After Exercises Fox and Dog, the commanders learned that the divisions needed more training on moving together to ensure that traffic jams did not occur. By the time the division participated in Exercise Bumper, the traffic problems were almost gone.

While large scale exercises were taking place every few months in 1941, there was also another type of training that became particularly popular during this time: battle drill. Both

English and Stacey describe the concepts of battle drill and the Canadians response to it. Stacey described battle drill as the reduction of military tactics to bare essentials, which were taught to a platoon as a team drill, with clear explanations regarding the objects to be achieved, the principles involved, and the individual task of each member of the team.[38] The Canadians immediately embraced battle drill training. There were different practice skills emphasised in the battle drill, everything from infiltration to platoon movements, to attacking enemy posts and pillboxes. Soldiers also practiced advanced assault training. These courses built on from what the soldiers learned in the battle drill course. There was more focus on firing different weapons, attacking, and patrols.[39] One of the battle drill courses that were completed by the 1st Canadian Division Infantry Reinforcement Unit consisted of everything from battle lectures, guerilla warfare, night patrols, carrier driving, to close combat to fighting in different surroundings.[40] So it appears reinforcement troops in replacement units carried out the same training as units in the field army.

Battle inoculation was also introduced during these battle drills. The aim of this training was to prepare soldiers "mentally and psychologically" to withstand the harsh realities of the battlefield.[41] This consisted of exposing men to live fire at close range in a highly controlled environment. Captain Harold MacDonald, of the North Shore (NB) Regiment, described his inoculation of fire: "the first 50 feet you're afraid they'll hit you & the next 50 ft. you're praying that they will hit you."[42] MacDonald's instructors fired rifle and Bren light machine guns at him and his course mates during training. Some instructors set out to either to impress the soldiers with exhibitions of their own toughness or to frighten candidates beyond repair instead of conditioning the men to battle noises and dangers during battle.[43]

Copp argues that battle drill transformed the attitudes towards training and helped to invigorate the training cycle.[44] Training was becoming boring for the men and battle drill changed the way the men thought about training. While English maintains that battle drill was beneficial, he argues that battle inoculation was taken to the extreme and that it was not effective in simulating the actual conditions of the battlefield. He contends that more attention should have been spent on teaching soldiers to identify weapons and their locations through listening and observation.[45]

Carvell went to Britain with the intentions of joining the Carleton and York Regiment, however, upon his arrival he was transferred to the 1st Canadian Division Infantry Reinforcement Unit (1 C.D.I.R.U.) at Camp Whitley 101, just outside of Guilford, England.[46] The regiment was full when Carvell arrived; therefore, he was placed in the reinforcement unit until a position opened. When the war broke out and the soldiers were sent to Britain, the Canadian government continued to recruit for the regiments and to provide reinforcements. Once the regiments had reached their maximum number of soldiers, new recruits were placed in reinforcement units. According to Stacey, the training of reinforcements was a different problem and required a special organization.[47] Once troops began being sent overseas, centres were established to begin training the reinforcements. Fourteen training centres were established across Canada—five infantry (rifle), two infantry (machine guns), and the other arms and services had one centre each.[48] Training the reinforcement units commenced on 15 January 1940. In 1942, there was an increased demand for reinforcements to complete the First Canadian Army, and the divisions were for home defence.

The reinforcement units in Britain, originally known as holding units, underwent major organizational revisions throughout the course of the war. However, the commanders noticed that the morale of the soldiers was poor because of the name of the unit. The term 'holding unit' gave the impression that the soldiers were not a part of a real regiment, but were just being held until a space was available for them. The reinforcement units were originally formed to hold the soldiers until they could go into the regular regiments; however, they quickly were tasked to train the drafts arriving from Canada.[49]

The reinforcement units were also assuming responsibility for the defence of Britain when the regular units were on the large-scale exercises.[50] For example, the No. 2 "Wolf" Battalion was created in 1942 from the 1 C. D. I. R. U. This battalion was created to cover the positions of the 1st Battalion 48th Highlanders of Canada so they could participate in Exercise Tiger.[51] The diary stated that nothing unusual took place during the take over and the battalion continue to do drill exercises while on guard. During some of the exercises, some members of the reinforcement units were able to actively participate. Officers from the 7th Canadian Infantry Reinforcement Unit were sent to be umpires for Exercise Spartan.[52] Carvell trained with the 1 C. D. I. R. U. until 1943, when he was taken on strength with the 7th Canadian Infantry Reinforcement Unit (7 C. I. R. U.) on 1 February 1943.[53] The 7 C. I. R. U. was established as a new unit for the regiments from the Maritime Provinces (Cape Breton Highlanders, North Nova Scotia Highlanders, West Nova Scotia Regiment, Carleton and York Regiment, North Shore New Brunswick Regiment, and Princess Louise Fusiliers);[54] however, drafts from other provinces eventually started coming into this unit. In September 1943, they received many Royal Winnipeg Rifles and artillery personnel due to the new Infantry Corps arrangement of letting non-Maritime regiments into this unit.[55] Training occurred daily. Some days training was only for half the day, and Sunday's religious observation occurred. Drafts drifted in and out of the unit constantly being posted with the regular regiments. These constant changes made unity difficult. Soldiers from the regular regiments would also spend time in the reinforcement units after spending time in the hospital before joining their regiment again.[56] The reinforcement unit also participated in mock enemy attack exercises to ensure they were ready for combat.[57]

Carvell spent from October 1942 until February 1943 at the Canadian Training School in Borden, England and returned in September 1943. He completed many courses, including receiving his truck license and received the rank of Acting Lance Corporal. In March 1944, Carvell asked to be transferred to another unit for a change after spending over a year at the

Training School and 7 C. I. R. U.[58] He was placed with the Royal Winnipeg Rifles. He reverted to private at his own request in order to be transferred into the Winnipegs.[59] He stated that he wanted a change asked for the transfer to the unit.[60] Carvell's higher rank was not needed in the unit; by reverting to private; he was able to transfer into the unit. It was during this time that he started training for Operation Overlord with his comrades.

CHAPTER SEVEN

LIFE IN BRITAIN: TRAINING AND BOREDOM

Life for Canadian soldiers in Britain was more than just training. There were numerous activities that the soldiers could participate in the camps and on leave. The commanding officers quickly realized that the soldiers needed activities to occupy their time off, or they would find trouble, such as drinking, fighting, and crime. The winter of 1941-42 marked the low point for the Canadians in Britain due to the boredom and discontent demonstrated from the soldiers.[61] Letters home spoke of the discontent and the wanting to be in battle.

Auxiliary Services were organizations that provided care and resources for Canadian soldiers overseas. The Canadian government chartered four aid organizations to be responsible for the soldier's comforts while in Britain. These organizations were the Young Men's Christian Association (YMCA), the Canadian Legion, the Salvation Army, and the Knights of Columbus. The main effort of these organizations was directed toward giving Canadians places to go where they could be surrounded with comforting familiarities and be protected from the unhealthy influences that beckoned in any big city.[62]

These Auxiliary services also organized a great deal of rec-reation for the troops. Sports and games, always played around the camps, were significant in keeping up the morale of the soldiers up. A report from the 1st Canadian Division described that the playing of sports eliminated to a large extent the cause of trouble in towns and villages and contributed to an improve-ment in the troops' state of mind and physical fitness.[63] The soldiers did everything from rowing and softball to skating and golf. They would often invite the local children to play softball and baseball with them.[64] Carvell enjoyed playing softball and generally played infield. When he joined the 1st Canadian Infantry Division Reinforcement Unit, they started the month of July off with the observation of Dominion Day (Canada Day) which included a sports day and a dance that evening.[65] It was important that the soldiers were still able to celebrate Canadian holidays while they were overseas because they needed that connection with home. Often there were sport competitions between the different units that the soldiers took very seriously.[66] These competitions became highly organized and occurred on a large scale. Competitions were between the Canadian forces as well as the British and United States forces. Softball and boxing were two of the most popular sports. Even if the soldiers could not play, they would watch. Spectating was almost as popular as playing the sports themselves.[67]

Auxiliary Services performed many tasks besides promoting sports. They ran singsongs, bingo games, quiz programs, amateur shows, and bridge, cribbage, and darts tournaments.[68]They also provided stationery to soldiers, distributed free cigarettes, operated mobile canteens, and organized reading and writing rooms and libraries. They also organized other activities such as concerts, dances, films, and church services. Films were often shown once a week.[69] Soldiers were also allowed to attend entertainment shows in the homes of citizens in town.[70] Church services, both Catholic and Protestant, were held at the camp each Sunday. Some soldiers would attend services at the local churches instead of staying at the camps, and the congregations welcomed them.[71]

While the soldiers had numerous activities to participate in at the camps, the British cities lured many men on leave. Scotland was also a popular place to visit. There was always a strong Canadian presence in London. Many soldiers just wanted to spend time with a family, in a normal family home. They wanted to remember what life was like before the war. The British people opened their homes to these men because many of their own husbands/brothers/sons that were fighting with the British military and they wanted to take care of the Canadians since they could not take care of their own men. Many of the Canadians became almost like family to these British families who took them in. Any little piece of home helped the soldiers cope with being away. Many waited for letters and packages.

Carvell often received letters from his sisters and mother, and he often came back to camp after leave to mail from his family "I suppose there will be some mail for me when I go back to camp" he wrote to his sister, Pearl, 8 June 1943. "I had one from Thelma not long ago and one from Mum. I never hear from Ruth I dont know what is the matter with her she did write quite often."[72] He would write to his family about what life was like in Britain and send pictures and souvenirs for his young niece.[73]

Nothing was more vital to the morale of the soldiers abroad than mail. Mail originally moved quickly, but as the war continued there were delays and lost mail due to planes and ships being destroyed.[74] Canadians were always seeing familiar faces while they were in the cities even though the cities were large. Carvell, while on a nine-day leave, spent some time in London. While he was there, he met one of his childhood friends, William (Bill) Smith.[75] He wrote to his sister, Pearl, about this meeting saying "I met Bill Smith over here the other day he is looking fine but is quite thin I heard Eleanor [Smith's sister] was married."[76] Smith had enlisted two years before Carvell and joined the North Shore (NB) Regiment after arriving in Britain. While both Carvell and Smith arrived in Britain in 1942, Smith had spent two years training in Nova Scotia before going overseas.[77] It would have been by chance that they would have met in London, both on leave. However, they were able to enjoy each other's company and reminisce about home.

There were many activities in the cities for the soldiers and opportunities to meet new people. Spending time with the British women became a popular pastime for the Canadian soldiers. Romances quickly blossomed.[78] The Canadians took the women dancing, escorted them home, went to cinemas, and played bingo.[79] Many courtships started. Once the courtship began, the couples often would go on long walks, picnics, and boating. The pressing urgency of events and the realization that each day had to be lived to its fullest gave these war-time romances a passion and intensity that remained with those who experienced them for the rest of their lives.[80] Carvell had a girlfriend, Gladys Pullinger, in Brighton, who he would visit while he was on leave.[81]

While many of the courtships did result in marriage, Carvell did not marry his girlfriend. Within the first two and a half years that the Canadians were there, more than 5000 British women married Canadians.[82] There were regulations placed on the soldiers who wanted to marry their British girlfriends. All men under the age of twenty were required to get permission from their commanding officer, to marry, and any men under the age of nineteen needed written consent by their parents or guardians.[83] The majority of the women who married Canadians made new homes for themselves with their husbands in the Dominion, although some returned after a few months or years because they missed their mothers and families and could not endure the loneliness.

Life was not all rosy for the Canadians in Britain. Due to the lack of action, many soldiers questioned why they were there and why they could not be back home. When morale fell, soldiers found trouble and ended up on the bad side of the military and civilian police. Discontent and dissatisfaction boiled over in petty acts of disobedience.[84] Jonathan Vance argues that the crime rate involving the Canadians was probably no higher than that of other soldiers, but it certainly got more publicity.[85] The war diaries of the reinforcement units describe discipline and court marshals within the units.

It was also a common occurrence for soldiers to be Absent Without Leave (AWOL). Carvell was charged with AWOL for being gone overnight. He was sentenced to ten days confined to the barracks and forfeited ten days' pay.[86] The family never knew that he had gone AWOL until I started reading his service file. It did not go into detail while he decided not to come back to camp; just that he was gone for the night and was confined to the barracks as a punishment. Drinking became a common problem for the

Canadians. Fighting was common, as well as other poor behaviour including rocking, damaging, or stealing cars; smashing windows; breaking into houses; and drunkenly falling asleep in local yards for residents to find.[87] There were also some reports of traffic accidents involving soldiers as they crashed into vehicles and knocked down cyclists and pedestrians. Crimes that the Canadians committed ranged from major crimes, including murder, to the innumerable petty misdemeanours.[88] Most problems with the law were due to drunkenness. However, as the war continued, drink became less of a serious problem.

CHAPTER EIGHT

CANADA IN ACTION: DIEPPE

The Canadians in Britain finally saw action in August 1942, when the 2nd Canadian Infantry Division went to Dieppe. The plan for the raid on the port of Dieppe originated in April 1942. The plan consisted of a frontal attack on the town of Dieppe, combined with flank attacks, and preceded by a heavy air bombardment. Tanks would also be employed on the main beach. The object of this raid, according to Stacey, was to destroy enemy defences, the aerodrome installations at St. Aubin, power stations, and other facilities, as well as removing secret documents from the Divisional Headquarter at Arques.[89] More recent scholarship by historian David O'Keefe has uncovered that one of the main objectives of the raid was to remove a German Enigma code machine and code books from a German naval intelligence headquarters in the town.[90] The British were desperate to acquire German intelligent documents, code books, and the Enigma encryption machine. The plan was refined and was increasingly heralded as a dress rehearsal for the eventual invasion of Europe. It would be a test of combined arms and inter-service cooperation, as well as a chance to challenge German defences.[91] The planners knew that casualties would be inevitable, especially since it was an attack from sea against a fortified port. They needed speed and surprise to carry the day.

The Canadians readily accepted the task of leading the raid. The 2nd Canadian Division and 1st Canadian Tank Brigade would provide almost 5000 out of the 6000 men for the operation. There were also British soldiers participating in the raid. The Canadians were growing restless for battle, and Dieppe would provide the opportunity for them to get their feet wet. The men went through intense training to get ready for this assault. They practiced moving to and from landing crafts, cliff scaling, unarmed combat, weapons training, and assaulting beaches. Operation Rutter (code name for the Dieppe Raid) was set for early July. Weather played a major role as to when the raid could take place. There were only a few days a month when conditions for an amphibious raid are suitable due to the moon and tide schedules. The weather would not cooperate and after postponing it for a few days, authorities cancelled the operation on 8 July. It would have been too difficult to get the soldiers on the beaches on time for the assault. Surprise and shock were vital to the success of the raid. The Canadians were disappointed that they were not going into battle.

Just shortly after the cancellation of Operation Rutter, the planners began questioning whether the operation could be re-launched. Thinking that the enemy though might have heard of the raid, would never suspect the planners of mounting it again, the British decided to attack Dieppe in August.[92] This operation would be called Jubilee. British Field Marshal Montgomery was upset that the operation was still occurring because he believed that the enemy would have learned about it since it was cancelled.[93] The Canadians began to feel uneasy about the raid; however, they did not feel that they could turn down the operation since they had asked to be a part of it and the inactivity of the Canadian Army during the time of war.

The plan for this operation changed slightly from the original. The heavy bombing and naval guns that were planned for the first operation were no longer going to be involved.[94] Both the navy and air force refused to use their limited resources for the operation, not wanting to lose any more of their ships and planes.

Operation Jubilee was slated to take place on 19 August. The Royal Hamilton Light Infantry and the Essex Scottish would land on the beach in front of the town of Dieppe (White and Red Beach). The infantry was to be supported by Churchill tanks of the Calgary Regiment. The Royal Regiment of Canada and the Black Watch (Royal Highland Regiment) would land north of the main beach at the village of Puys (Blue Beach). The South Saskatchewan

Regiment and the Queen's Own Cameron Highlanders of Canada would land south of Dieppe at Pourville (Green Beach). The British commandos were to knock out a series of costal battery positions and a secret reserve of 250 British Royal Marines would also be landing with the Canadians.[95]

The Canadians and British soldiers boarded their ships late 18 August to set sail early in the morning to face the German 302nd Infantry Division, who held the high ground that completely dominated the Dieppe area. From the onset, the plan for the raid unravelled. Shortly after setting sail, the Allied ships ran into a German coastal convoy. While the run-in was short lived, it alerted the enemy defenses, removing the element of surprise upon which the plan depended. It was also disastrous for the British commandos who were trying to land on the coast. Many never landed where they were supposed to.[96]

Figure 4: Puys, Blue Beach, 2014. Author's Personal Collection

Puys beach is a located in a narrow cove surrounded by cliffs that rise sixty metres high. The beach, itself, is only 200 metres long and consists of small rocks instead of the sand which is found on other French beaches. These rocks make it very difficult to walk on the beach let alone try to run in army boots.[97] The beach was also blocked by a 3.5-metre concrete seawall and dense coil barbed wire. With the Germans having the machine gun positions along the cliff, the Canadians needed to land in darkness so they were not visible. The objective for the Royal Regiment of Canada and the Black Watch on Puys Beach was to secure the beach and destroy the machine guns, heavy and light flank installations, and the gun battery. This needed to be achieved to ensure that the weapons could not fire on the main beach in front of Dieppe.[98]

The 554 Royals and 111 Black Watch landed approximately thirty minutes late and were fully visible to the German gun operators. While the Germans only had two platoons, approximately one hundred soldiers, they were easily able to ready themselves for the Canadian attack. The Canadians waited on the landing craft, their bodies and minds as honed by the training as they could be, but still ignorant of the raw savagery that only those who have endured real combat can understand. As soon as the landing craft lowered its ramp, mortar fire ripped through these strong, but inexperienced young soldiers. Many men died before even setting foot off the landing craft, forcing their comrades to climb over their bodies. Despite the fire, they had to keep going. They had a job to do, so they had to run right into the hail of mortar. Those who got onto the beach used the concrete wall for protection.

Even with their brethren dying all around them, the Royals continued to get off the landing crafts to their objective or risked their lives to save others. The second wave came about twenty minutes later and there was little that they could do but watch their comrades be mowed down. All that was added was the number of those killed. No information was sent back to the ships; therefore, the next wave of soldiers, the Black Watch, came.[99] Waves of mortar fire cut them down in a bloody mass, staining the sand and stones red.[100] A small group of Royals were able to get off the beach and hoped to meet with the Essex Scottish; however, they didn't get to the Scottish, and they had to surrender. The Essex Scottish Regiment landed on the main Dieppe on Red Beach. They were pinned down on the beach by fire and only a small group was able to get off the beach to continue to their objective.

No one was prepared for the carnage that occurred on Puys. The Royals finally surrendered at 0830, three hours after the assault started. Two hundred and twenty-seven Royals were killed out of the 554 who landed. Only sixty-seven men made it back to Britain, and the rest were taken prisoner.[101]

Figure 5: Pourville, Green Beach, 2014. Author's Personal Collection

The South Saskatchewan Regiment, landing at Pourville, had much more success than any other regiment during this raid. Pourville beach was much longer than Puys; however, it was still dominated by the cliffs on both sides. Unlike what happened at Puys, the South Saskatchewans landed when they were supposed to under the cover of darkness. The only mishap with the initial landings was that two companies were dropped off in the wrong place, dividing the regiment. Their objectives were to secure the town and capture the western headland overlooking the main beach.[102] The regiment was able to get on the beach and started making their way towards their objective. They were unable to secure their objectives due to the enemy defences and not having the artillery support. The Queen's Own Cameron Highlanders of Canada also landed at Pourville, after the South Saskatchewans. They took heavy enemy fire while in the landing crafts. Once they were able to get on the beach, they pushed inland toward a series of houses. They came under severe enemy hire and the casualties were high. By 0930 hours, orders to withdraw to the landing crafts came. Six hundred out of the 1200 men who landed made it back to Britain.[103]

Puys and Pourville needed to be secured for the landing on the main beach of Dieppe to be successful. The main beach of Dieppe was 1.6 kilometres long. White Beach stretched over half a kilometre from the western headland and Red Beach extended east to the harbour mouth. The Royal Hamilton Light Infantry would land on White Beach and the Essex Scottish would land on Red Beach. Nine Calgary Regiment tanks would land alongside the infantry for fire support. The landing was to take place on 0520 hours.[104]

Naval bombardment pounded the Dieppe fortifications, but the bombings did not help. Many of the Germans were hiding in the hotels, tobacco factory, and churches. None of the defences had been destroyed and the tanks were late arriving. The infantry went in cold and without the element of surprise. The Germans were on full alert after the landings at Puys and Pourville. Many landing crafts hit mines, and were shot by machine guns, and mortar fire.

Of all the German weaponry used that day, mortar fire was the deadliest, according to historian Tim Cook.[105] The Essex Scottish tried to make their landing at Red Beach. The men who were able to get out of the landing crafts tried to take cover as soon as they hit the beach. They tried to organize themselves to continue with their objectives; however, German snipers picked off Non-Commissioned Officers (NCOs) and officers who were coordinating the advance. Only a small group of Essex made it off the beach to continue with their plan.

The Royal Hamilton Light Infantry fared better than the Essex Scottish. They were able get off the beach and were able to press into the casino overlooking the Promenade. The Royal Hamiltons continued to advance until they were low on ammunition. They had to retreat to the beach. During this time, there was mass confusion, and information was not getting back to the ships and the commanding officers. The Fusiliers Mont-Royal were sent into battle because they commanding officers thought the Essex Scottish and Royal Hamiltons had pushed into the town. The Fusiliers landed at 0700 hours. Few made it through the fire zone. Those who did took cover where they could.[106]

The withdrawal of the troops from the beaches was set to take place at 1100 hours. Landing crafts came in to bring the men back to the ships. There was naval and air force fire support to cover the withdrawals. Men tried to get back to the ships; however, very few made it back. Four hundred men made it back to the ships.[107] At 1400 hours, the shooting stopped. Those still on shore surrendered to the Germans.

The Dieppe Raid turned out to be a tactical disaster. Out of the attacking force of nearly 5000, 907 died on the beach, 1946 were captured, and 586 were wounded.[108] The raid was an awful sacrifice for the Canadians.

Eventually, the shock of losing so many men wore off, and morale and the focus on training increased. Though the blood of nine hundred men stained the beach of Dieppe, the job was not complete, and they had to keep fighting. The Canadians knew that they needed to be better prepared to fight the Germans.

Chapter Nine

Preparing for Normandy

In 1943, the Americans and British decided that a cross Channel attack into France would take place in the spring of 1944, called Operation Overlord. From the onset of planning, the invasion would be a joint American-Canadian-British operation with equal measures.[109] The 1st Canadian Infantry Division went to Italy in the summer of 1943. The Canadian government wanted their troops to gain combat experience but also still get back to Britain in time for any landings in France.

Milner argues that the British supported more Canadian involvement in the Italian campaign to ensure that the British would take on a more prominent role in the Normandy landings than was initially planned. The original plan saw the Americans leading the invasion with the Canadians as their breakout force. This meant that the Second British Army would not come into the battle until much later, which would leave them out of the critical moment in the war in the west.[110] The British believed they needed to be one of the main attacking forces in the liberation of Europe. The Canadian government offered no objection to sending more troops to Italy so they could fight on a larger scale, even though that would impact Canada's role in France. Once General McNaughton was removed from command of the First Canadian Army in December 1943, the British would receive the prominent role in the invasion that they wanted.

One of the first tasks facing the planners of Operation Overlord was where it would take place. The Pas de Calais and the Cotentin-Caen (Normandy) area were the two possible choices. They both had advantages and disadvantages. Pas de Calais was only twenty miles (thirty kilometres) from the coast of Britain, which promised optimum air support and a quick turn-around of shipping. The beaches also had a high capacity. The main disadvantage was that the area was heavily fortified because the Germans believed an invasion would take place there. The Cotentin-Caen area was further from Britain, therefore, reducing the amount of air support. A longer sea voyage would complicate the naval problems. The advantages of this area were that the German defences were light, the beaches had a very high capacity, and the area provided exceptionally suitable ground for the rapid development of forward airfields close to the coast.[111] General D. Eisenhower, the Supreme Allied Commander, knew that for a cross-Channel attack to be successful, they would need to go in force. It would also be a joint effort between the army, air force, and navy; the air force and navy would provide the bombardments needed for the infantry to take the beaches.

The Caen sector was a part of the German's Atlantic Wall. This was the 4500-kilometre coastline of France. Hitler had fortified the French coast for four years with thousands of defensive installations, from concrete bunkers to hundreds of machine gun and artillery encasements and some 4.2 million mines in the water and beaches.[112] The Atlantic Wall boasted a defence of sixty infantry divisions; however, many were burnt out from the battles on the Eastern Front. The Germans also had numerous panzer (armoured vehicles and tank) divisions that could destroy the invasion if they were not held. There were four panzer and one panzer grenadier division that were full strength and battle ready within the Caen sector.[113] The most immediate danger was the 12th SS Panzer Division (Hitler Youth). It had 23,000 personnel, and it was equipped with transport and armoured vehicles, with over-strength infantry companies led by a battle-hardened cadre of youthful Nazi fanatics from the 1st SS Panzer Division.[114] Hitler was also in charge to releasing the panzer divisions during an invasion, to the indignation of battlefield generals, who wanted to be in charge of releasing these divisions themselves instead of having to wait until Hitler gave the official word.

The number of divisions landing during the Normandy invasion changed throughout the planning stages. The original plan called for three divisions landing, one for each country. The planners realized that more divisions would be needed in order to take the beaches. They changed the number to six divisions. This gave the Americans and British each an additional beach to overcome. The Canadians would take one beach, since they did not have the troops to take more.[115] The six Allied divisions would assault an eighty-kilometre front on five discontinuous beaches.[116]

The 1st US Army was to land west of Bayeux astride the Vire River inlet. The western flank was to be secured by two US airborne divisions, the 101st and the 82nd. They would destroy several major coastal gun batteries exits for 4th US Infantry Division, which was to land on a long strip of dunes dubbed Utah Beach. US Rangers were to assault the gun position at Pointe du Hoc. The main American landing was made by the 1st US Division and elements of the 29th US Division on Omaha Beach. Omaha was one of the toughest beaches due to its natural landscape of tall bluffs. The Germans added more obstacles to make getting off the beach more difficult.[117]

Figure 6: The cliffs of Pointe du Hoc, 2014.
Author's Personal Collection

Figure 7: Omaha Beach, 2014. Standing at the water's edge
looking up to the landing of the Americans.
Author's personal collection

The British were to land on Gold Beach, twenty kilometres from Omaha Beach. The 50th British Division and XXX British Corps were to land there. Gold allowed them to take the crucial small ports of Arromanches and Port-en-Bessin, providing direct access to the road to Bayeux.

A short gap from Gold was Juno Beach, where the 3rd Canadian Division would land. The area was characterized by seafront villages along a low waterline. Courseulles-sur-Mer was guarded by a series of large concrete emplacements right at the waterline. The strongpoint there made it the toughest beach after Omaha. Bernieres-sur-Mer was heavily defended by machine gun positions and antitank guns. St. Aubin-sur-Mer had more strong points that had to be overcome.[118]Just another short gap from Juno was Sword, the last beach. The 3rd British Division was to land on this highly defended space.

The Overlord front extended over eighty kilometres. The plan called for it to be taken by more than 150,000 troops landing on the first day with thousands more landing in the days after.[119] It was planned by the end of the day on 6 June, that more than 21,000 Canadians would be ashore, with over 2000 vehicles.[120] With the plans in place, the training for the invasion began.

The battalions involved in the invasion changed their training program in 1943 from defending against invasion to invasion operations. The training for Overlord would be completed in four phases. The first phase would be the preliminary training which involved the study of principles of combined operations and practice in embarkation and disembarkation, scaling obstacles, and clearing minefields. The second phase was on the mechanics of assault landings. The third phase was increased realism with the assault training, and the final phase was collective divisional assault training.[121]

By the beginning of 1944, the Winnipegs, who George Carvell would soon join, were training in all phases. The training now focused on overcoming the beach defences and rapidly advancing to and seizing a series of objects.[122] Companies completed assault landing training as well as battle drill, mine clearing practice, education on the German Army, combined operations, and inoculation parades. Map reading, semaphore practice, cross country runs, cliff scaling, assault landing drill, and PIAT (Projector, Infantry, Anti-Tank) firing were also routine in the pre-D-Day months.[123] This routine training was rotated each day through the month. Inspections, sports, and church services took place on the weekends. January saw lectures and sand table exercises on infantry-tank cooperation conducted jointly with the 1st Hussars from the 2nd Canadian Armoured Brigade.[124]

At the end of January, the Winnipegs participated in Exercise Cordage, designed to give the various supporting arms, as used in assault landings, an opportunity to practice firing their weapons according to a prearranged fire plan on chosen targets.[125] February consisted of most of the same training as January. The regiment did participate in more divisional exercises throughout the month. Headquarters participated in Exercise Flash, a theoretical 3rd Division advance against theoretical German forces in defended localities.[126] Lectures on the German army and weapons occurred throughout the month. A sniper school was also established. Near the end of the month, the regiment participated in Exercise Sodamint. It was a combined operation of forces landing exercise where the companies were to push inland and clear the beaches. The war diary states that the Winnipegs were successful in their objective in this exercise. General Montgomery came to inspect the 7th

Brigade. He also spent time speaking to the men to build confidence and inspire them.

When Carvell joined the Winnipegs in March 1944, he filled a vacant infantry private position in the Winnipegs that was possibly created from a training injury, a problem, or a medical transfer or illness. He willingly gave up his rank of Acting Lance Corporal to transfer to this regiment and in hopes of going into battle sooner. Carvell had the challenge of proving himself and integrating into a tight-knit unit that had been training together for nearly four years and only a few months to accomplish this. His experience was not unique; it represented the experience of hundreds of other reinforcements transferred into well-established units in the last months before they embarked for the front. When Carvell joined in March, the Winnipegs continued the same training that they had been doing in January and February.

April training was slightly different. The month began with the regiment receiving orders that they would be moving to sealed camps in just a few days. After the camp move, they began preparations for Exercise Trousers, a D-Day landing exercise.[127] Before leaving for the exercise, the regiment attended a lecture on the treatment of Prisoners of War (POWs).[128] B and D Companies participated, and they had a reserve company with them. Their objective was to land on the beaches and travel six miles inland.[129] The companies did well. They were able to climb the cliffs, proceed to wipe out the imaginary forces, and push to the first report line which signaled the completion of phrase one. They continued with the other three phases, achieving their report lines without problems.[130] The month was also the 61st anniversary of the founding of the RWR, so they celebrated the anniversary. His Majesty King George VI came to visit the regiment. He strolled slowly through the battalion, so the men could see him up close. His appearance was a source of strength and inspiration to them.[131] At the end of April, Carvell was placed in the 10 Platoon of B Company to continue with his training for the invasion.

May was the last month of training before the D-Day invasion. The Winnipegs moved camps once again, and security roadblocks sprang up around the camp. The regiments involved in the invasion were soon sequestered until they went into battle. The regiment participated in Exercise Fabius, which was a mock run of the initial landings and the push inland.[132] The rest of the month consisted of preparations for Operation Overlord. All leaves were cancelled. Company commanders received final briefings on the operation. General Eisenhower came to address the 7th Brigade on 13 May, speaking for about ten minutes in order to boost morale.[133] Due to the fact most of the soldiers going into this invasion had never seen battle before, the brigade sent battle notes describing elements such as mines, booby traps, patrols, attack, and defense.[134]

The original date of the invasion was 5 June. The last few days before the invasion were busy for all involved. The Winnipegs were split into major assault craft loads and started moving some of the companies to the ships. They were issued with 24-hour ration packs, emergency chocolate, vomit bags (for use on the small assault craft), water sterilizing tablets, and all other necessary equipment to make the individual self-contained for the first forty-eight hours after landings.[135] Once the battalion was aboard the ships, the soldiers just had to wait until it was time for the invasion.

CHAPTER TEN

D-DAY AND JUNO BEACH

The Normandy invasion has gone down in history as one of the pivotal moments of the Second World War. Nobody involved would ever completely forget what they witnessed and endured. They saw loss, but they also saw victory, courage, and strength. Each soldier had a different D-Day experience, but those who survived would have the experiences of this day etched into their minds for the rest of their lives, including George Carvell.

Canadians, Americans, British, and Frenchmen began to achieve the liberation of France. General Eisenhower spent months orchestrating this invasion, even postponing it a day due to the weather. For some Canadian units, including the Royal Winnipeg Rifles, the invasion was the culmination of four years of training in Britain and finally a chance to fight the enemy.

For Rifleman George Carvell, the Normandy invasion and the Battle of Putot-en-Bessin would be life-changing. After spending two years training in Britain, he would finally meet the enemy and get a taste of combat. Though he did not know it in those nerve-wracking days leading up to the invasion, his active service would be mercifully short-lived, as he joined the many other men who were captured during those first few days of fighting. He would also confront the murderous nature of the 12th SS Hitler Youth Panzer Division. The original date for the D-Day invasion was set for 5 June 1944. The soldiers from the assault units were sequestered together from late-May until the date of the invasion due to security reasons.[136] The commanders did not want a repeat of Dieppe; therefore, security was the upmost importance. Due to poor weather, General Eisenhower decided to postpone the invasion for twenty-four hours. The soldiers waited anxiously in the ships, trying to find things to do before they were finally told to board the assault crafts. Corporal Cecil Lelonde of D Company of the Winnipegs recalled playing cards and gambling to pass the time.[137] Nearly all men wrote letters to their loved ones. The letters were supposed to be sent out later; however, many of the soldiers found out after the war that these letters were never sent at all.[138]

General Eisenhower gave the official notice that the invasion would take place on 6 June. Final preparations for the invasion began. At 2100 hours, the ships, some containing the Winnipegs, sailed to meet their escorts. The ranks were finally told they were going to the coast of France, briefed on live maps, and given final orders.[139] Final preparations were also made with the supporting groups to the infantry. Even with the twenty-four-hour postponement, the waters were still quite rough and many of the men were sick. The soldiers were awake by 0330 to have breakfast and a church service.[140] The weather also was not ideal for the airborne drops that would be taking place before the infantry landed on the beaches due to the wind. Most did not end up where they were supposed to land.[141] The air power attack also failed to get the expected results.[142] The naval attack failed to bring the level of destruction to the fortifications on the beaches that the Overlord planers envisioned.

The 3rd Canadian Infantry Division would lead the Canadians into the Normandy invasion. The 7th Canadian Infantry Brigade, the Royal Winnipeg Rifles, the Regina Rifles, and the Canadian Scottish Regiment (Can-Scots), landed on Nan Green beach, Mike Red, and Mike Green beach at Courseulles-sur-Mer. The 8th Canadian Infantry Brigade, the Queen's Own Rifles, the North Shore (New Brunswick) Regiment, and le Regiment de la Chaudière, landed on Nan White and Nan Red beach at Bernieres-sur-Mer and Saint-Aubin. The 9th Canadian Infantry Brigade would follow on the reserve brigade. The infantry would be supported by naval bombardments and the air force. The 2nd Armoured Brigade and specialized vehicles would also be landing on the beaches with infantry.

The Canadians were the last of the Allies to arrive to their beach that morning, arriving ten minutes late. The Royal Winnipeg Rifles were the first to land at 0750 hours. To the left of the Winnipegs, the Regina Rifles landed at 0800 hours against the eastern part of Coureulles-sur-Mer. B Squadron, the 1st Hussars, were supposed to land nineteen tanks before the Reginas in support; however, five never made it while the others were swept eastward. The Reginas suffered losses before ever getting out of their landing crafts. Two of the crafts hit mines in the water, killing fifty men instantly.[143]

A Company landed right in front of the Courseulles strongpoint. The company had an assault strength of 119 men, and they tackled the beach defences alone. They were supposed to have the support of the tanks; however, B Company ended up with the tank support. It took most of the morning for them to clear the beach and lower Courseulles. By noon, eighty men lay dead or wounded.[144] B and C Companies had a much easier landing than A Company. The Reginas advanced to their next objectives until they dug in at Le Fresne-Camilly for the night.

The Queen's Own Rifles of Canada, of the 8th Canadian Infantry Brigade, landed on Nan White beach at Bernieres-sur-Mer. The landing plan was for A Company to land on the right of the town, and B Company would land on the left. They were to be supported by the tanks from Fort Garry Horse, which were to land before the men to help take out any strong points that were not destroyed during the pre-invasion bombardment. The tanks were late arriving; therefore, the companies had to go in cold, without the extra gun fire. To make matters worse, the storm had caused problems, and they landed in front of the town instead of its sides. The heavily fortified town had to be taken by direct assault across about fifty meters of flat, wet land.[145] The war diary states that the companies would wait an additional thirty minutes before landing. Though there is no official reason for this, the basic assumption is that it was because the tanks were late.[146]

A Company landed exactly at 0812, in front of a German 88mm anti-tank gun that survived the bombardment and had not shown up on the pre-invasion reconnaissance.[147] The men were cut down by heavy fire. One platoon of A Company was left with five men unwounded out of one hundred and nineteen. One LCA lost ten out of the first eleven men who tried to get out of the craft to machine gun fire. D Company landed in the same area and lost half of its 119 men running to the seawall. The deadly fire continued until three riflemen took the bunker with hand grenades. A Company left forty dead and wounded on the beach before they could continue the advance.[148]

B Company's experience was very similar to A Company. They were blown off course, and they landed in front of four concrete pillboxes housing machine guns. Within the first few minutes of the battle, there were sixty-five casualties.[149] C Company landed fifteen minutes after the initial landings. There was still heavy fire that they needed to overcome before meeting with the other companies. Battalion Headquarters arrived at 0900 hours, and the companies assembled together at 0940 hours before pushing into Bernieres-sur-Mer.[150] The regiment consolidated and continued their advance. They followed the La Regiment de la Chaudiere into Beny-sur-Mer. Once Beny was clear, C and D Company, with the tanks, quickly moved to their final objective of Anguerny. They encountered a small band of resistance in the village that they overcome and taking prisoners.[151] They dug in for the night at this position. For the Queen's Own Rifles, D-Day came at tremendous cost. The regiment lost sixty-one men, and another seventy-six were wounded, the most of any Canadian regiment that day.

While the Queen's Own Rifles was landing at Nan White, the North Shore (New Brunswick) Regiment was landing at Nan Red. Their objective was the strong point on Cap Romain at St. Aubin. The North Shore's A Company and B Company landed first at 0810 hours. A Company landed immediately west of St. Aubin-sur-Mer and pass through an open gap between this town and Bernieres-sur-Mer. B Company pushed directly into St. Aubin. The companies were supported by the Fort Garry Horse.

A Company landed and got through the defences quickly with few casualties. They did not suffer higher casualties until they reached the town houses. B Company was faced with a much harder landing. They landed in front of a strong point that has not been destroyed by the air and naval bombardment.[152] They were trapped on the beach from the gunfire. They called on for the tanks to help them clear out the point, so they could continue on to their objective.[153] C and D Companies came ashore and had little trouble in the beginning.

The Royal Marines joined the North Shores and pushed into the town of St. Aubin. They found the town full of tunnels, trenches, and gun positions.[154] It was a well-defended area and snipers were a major issue once in town. However, they took St. Aubin by 1115 hours. One platoon, approximately thirty-seven men, was left in the town to finish the job of finding all the snipers while the others continued to their next objective, Tailleville. C Company led the advance with A Company following. With the help of the tanks, they were able to clear the area. They found a fully developed coastal defence system once they were in the village. Fighting in Tailleville was stalled, and they decided to regroup and continue the following day.

The reserve unit for the North Shore and Queen's Own Rifles was La Regiment de la Chaudiere. They landed on Nan White at 0830 hours, fifteen minutes after the Queen's Own Rifles had landed. The rising sea covered many of the obstacles that were on the beach, making it difficult to disembark. Many of the men stripped off their equipment and swam to the shore with only their knives to fight with.[155] The Chauds spent time on the beach waiting for the Queen's Own Rifles clear Bernieres. They could not continue with the advance until the strong points were taken out. This delay also delayed the reserve brigade from landing on the beach and advancing to their objective. Once they got through the town, they stayed at their assembly area for two hours before finally continuing their advance southwest towards Beny-sur-Mer. With the support of Fort Garry Horse, they were able to take Beny-sur-Mer within an hour, which gave the 9th Canadian Infantry Brigade the ability to continue to their objective of Carpiquet.

Each Canadian regiment faced a hardened German army in the hopes of breaking through Hitler's Atlantic Wall. The British were unable to take Caen the first day which affected the Canadian objectives. However, they were still able to achieve more in one day than the Allies had managed in the previous several years.

CHAPTER ELEVEN

THE ROYAL WINNIPEG RIFLES

The Royal Winnipeg Rifles were the first Canadian regiment to land on Juno Beach. George Carvell was in the 10th Platoon of B Company, which was one of the first companies to land that day. The Winnipegs were ten miles from the coast when they were given the order for the Landing Craft Assault (LCAs) to be manned and lowered from the ships. The Winnipeg's war diary stated that at 0655 hours that no shots had come from ashore, everything was quiet until the naval bombardment began.[156] At 0749 hours, C Company of the 1st Canadian Scottish Regiment landed at the juncture of Mike and Love for the assault on beach defense and the Chateau Vaux. D Company of the Winnipegs, commanded by Major Fulton, landed to the left on Mike Green and B Company, commanded by Captain Gower, landed on Mike Red.[157]

The Winnipegs faced massive, unexpected obstacles right from the start. Tanks of A Squadron of the 1st Hussars were supposed to land with the Winnipegs for support; however, only seven of the tanks made it to the beaches, and they were late arriving.[158] To make matters worse, the naval bombardment had failed to kill a single German or silence one weapon. The support fire fell either short or long of the German positions.

Between the late tanks and the naval bombardment's failure to take out the German weapons, the Winnipegs went in cold, without support. Captain Gower and his men of B Company faced an unbelievable task. They were confronted with three large bunkers, at least twelve machine gun positions, and a network of trenches and wire.[159] It was going to be brutal, and it was going to be bloody, but Gower led his men forward with great resolve because there was no other choice but to press on.

They, like every other unit that had landed on Normandy's shores, had a job to do. Beginning when the LCAs were 700 yards from the beach, B Company encountered heavy machine gun, shell, and mortar fire.

To get onto the beach, the men had to disembark from the landing crafts while chest-deep in the sea.[160] Weakened from being seasick and weighed down with extra weapons, communication gear, or ammunition, many men got hit before they even touched land, their blood staining the icy seawater.[161] Some men drowned, not even making the beach or battle. Others died from their wounds before their boots hit the beach. Rifleman Edward (Albert) Johnson, B Company, described his experience coming on the beach saying, "I landed on D-Day and had to advance through murderous fire from two machine gun posts which had been missed by the bombs and shells that fell on the beach ahead of us."[162] The men did everything they could to get on the beach. In situation that echoed painfully of Dieppe, many men did not even make it out of the LCAs before getting shot. The men of B Company quickly realized that not many of their company had gotten to the beach, and those who did were confronted with more fire power than expected.

My great-great Uncle George Carvell was in the midst of all this. He was a twenty-one-year-old timber man from New Brunswick who, just two years previously, had still lived in his mother's house, worn the clothes she'd sewn and mended for him, and eaten the fresh biscuits and butter that she'd made. Many of his fellow soldiers were even younger, some of them hardly growing facial hair. But they were strong, and they were brave, and their bodies served perhaps the most vital purpose anyone could consider at the time—a physical and metaphorical shield between the horrors of Nazi domination and the gentle, warm-hearted communities these men loved in their homeland. One after another, they surged out of those landing crafts and into the free-for-all of mortar and bullets, aware that each breath might be the last they drew. For many, those last breaths came very soon.

My great-great uncle lived many decades after the war's end, but in all that time, he spoke very little of what took place when he landed on Juno Beach and the amount of fire they were under. I wish I knew what he thought or felt as he slipped into the water and moved toward the shore, most definitely seeing his comrades die around him, probably touching or stumbling over their bodies in his own struggle to reach land. I don't know if he was aware of the tremendous amount of firepower coming at him. Like most war veteran families, we had an understanding—there are things you simply do not ask.

Major Fulton and his men of D Company jumped off the LCAs into waist-deep water and struggled ashore at the same time as B Company. They were met with much less fierce opposition when disembarking because their landing was clear of the actual strongpoint area. Corporal Lelonde described what he saw and felt when first landing on the beach:

I don't recall hearing any firing or explosions. It's hard to explain, but it was as though I was drunk, maybe with fear. We just ran like hell, zigzagging like rabbits. I never saw a body fall and never saw any of the beach.[163]

For D Company, there was relatively little difficulty in gapping a minefield at La Valette and clearing the village of Graye-sur-Mer beyond it.

B Company, with the aid of the tanks that had finally arrived, eventually captured the pillboxes commanding the beach before forcing their way across the Seulles bridge and clearing the enemy positions on the island between the river and the little harbour.[164] There were at least, possibly more than, fifteen machine guns. The battalion also encountered five concrete emplacements by on the Courseulles beach. They took some of these enemy positions quickly; however, they had to fight some in hand-to-hand combat, getting up close and personal with the bodies and faces of their enemies.[165] For most of the men, Carvell included, this was the first time they'd been face to face with a German soldier. By 0900 hours, B Company had cleared their initial objectives, but not without major cost. The company had started with an assault strength of 119 men of all ranks; however, only Captain Gower and twenty-six men survived. One of these fortunate survivors was George Carvell.

When A Company, commanded by Major Hodge, and C Company, commanded by Major Jones, landed with half of Battalion Headquarters, they were still under heavy mortar and machine gun fire. They were pinned down for two hours on the beach.[166] Major Hodge and his men were able to push inland toward Ste. Croix-sur-Mer and reached just short of assaulting distance before they were pinned down by fire. Rifleman Tony Hubert of A Company described his experience landing on the beach: "the pillboxes were really active. We had problems getting the tanks ashore; flamethrowers were used. Then when the armour came in and we cleaned up this mess."[167]

Major Jones and his men advanced towards their objective Banville at 0900 hours. Two men were killed from the company when crossing the beach.[168] They encountered several pockets of resistance en route but overcame each one until just south of Banville. It was also at this time that the artillery arrived on the beaches and began firing in support. C and D Companies were able to take the village of Banville after hard fighting and support from the guns.

The first phase of the operation was complete with the taking of the village.

Even with the Winnipegs taking their first phase objectives, they did not reach them quickly enough for the Canadian Scottish Regiment to get their final objectives on the Caen-Bayeux highway. They would have to make up the time the next day to get the final objectives secured.

The initial beach landing provided many opportunities for bravery and heroism of the soldiers from the Winnipegs and memories that would never diminish. The war diary describes numerous incidences where the soldiers continued even after being mortally wounded. Reports tell of how, after being hit in the stomach, Corporal Slatter was on his hands and knees still trying to get up to the pillbox and directing his section by shouting orders. Corporal Klos was badly wounded in the stomach and legs; however, he was still able to make his way to the pillbox and kill two German soldiers before succumbing to his wounds.[169] Captain Gower was awarded the Military Cross for his leadership and bravery during the initial fighting.

Uncle George never spoke to the family about the Juno Beach landings. In 1994, after doing a veteran's tour for the 50th anniversary of the battle, he did an interview with the local paper where he described the landing on the beaches vividly. He recalled the crossing to be very rough that morning and said that if he'd had to be on the boat much longer he would have been sick. They could only go so far on the ships before the craft ramps were lowered. Then they waded ashore to the beach. His platoon officer was killed at the beginning of the invasion and left a sergeant in charge. He recalled that there was a lot of confusion during the initial landings; however, there was no time to be afraid.[170] That might have been the key to the incomprehensible bravery of those men who waded out into a hail of gunfire. They had a job to do; there was no time to think about fear. Their purpose was too great, the expectations and security of a nation resting on their young shoulders. Though our troops moved forward that day, and accomplished what they'd been sent to do, the experience was no fleeting one. Major Fulton stated that 6 June 1944 "is a day that will remain forever in the memories of those who survived."[171]

With the bravery and heroism shown during the first few hours of the landings, the Winnipegs and Can-Scots continued onto the second phase of the operation. By 1400 hours, all but A Company of the Winnipegs had made it to Banville as well as two squadrons from the 1st Hussars. C and D Companies had already moved out of Banville when B Company arrived. Battalion Headquarters reorganized before moving on to the next objective. B Company continued to press forward even though there were so few left in the company after the beach fighting. It was also during this time A Company asked for assistance with the enemy machine guns at Croix-sur-Mer. Portions of the armoured regiment went to A Company to help and they quickly took out the positions, so the company could continue with their advance to Creully.

The Winnipegs began consolidating in and around the village of Creully. They would stay there for the night and continue to their D-Day objective of Putot-en-Bessin the next day. There was little German resistance between Banville and Creully aside from one machine gun. Lieutenant Mitchell of D Company and a section of riflemen were able to silence the machine gun position.

As the evening approached, the reinforcements for the unit arrived. Five officers and seventy-eight other ranks all went into B Company.[172] Some of the men escorted German prisoners to the beach where, they were loaded onto ships to head back to Britain. Rifleman Hurbert recalled the sights he saw when back on the beach when escorting the prisoners:

[T]he boys were stacked four high in long rows—some half bodies, some tops missing, some blown to bits. You name it; everything was there. To this day in my vision. I can still see this. I shall never forget those who gave their all.[173]

While consolidating and digging into the position, the Winnipegs were still under constant fire. The companies were able to attend to the wounded and give them the best treatment they could give under the circumstances, which proved to be difficult with the constant German fire. Morale was also increasing from the strong showing of the men and being able to take care of their wounded. It was a statement to one another that yes, they could do this. They could face this horrifying ordeal and still be human enough afterward to care for one another's wounds.

After the day's fighting, the Winnipegs dug in for the night. Brigadier Harry Foster, commander of the 7th Brigade, convened an Orders Group for the 7th Canadian Infantry Brigade at 0130 hours, 7 June. The commanders received the marching orders for the day. The Winnipegs would start the advance at 0600 hours to their objective of Putot-en-Bessin. The Regina Rifles would make their advance just shortly after. Brigadier Foster hoped that the brigades would reach the Caen-Bayeux railway before the German counterattack.[174] At 0200 hours, enemy patrols attacked C Company. The company allowed the patrol to penetrate the company's defensive position. The company then encircled the patrol.[175] Successfully repelling the attack, the company took nineteen of the patrol as prisoners. They also took one officer; however, he was shot when he tried to escape.

As the first day of fighting came to a close, the war diary ended the day's account with a special note on the Battalion's effort that day. It stated that "not one man flinched from his task, no matter how tough it was—not one officer failed to display courage and energy and a degree of gallantry."[176] The Winnipegs showed great strength despite the difficulties that they faced. This was common among all the battalions that landed on Juno Beach that day. Each regiment met great difficulties; however, they were not deterred by these difficulties. They had kept going, achieving their goals and getting the job done, beginning that massive sweep that was to take back the Western Front from German occupation. It was no small victory. This day, this harrowing, bloody, brutal day that they spent the last few years training and preparing for, was finally over, and they begun to turn the tide of the war.

The cost of the invasion, though, was high. The Winnipegs had over 130 casualties on their roster, with the majority coming from B Company, George Carvell's company. As they rested that night, they didn't know what would await them at dawn, except for more fighting. They didn't know that their numbers would soon be decimated further, and that they would come face to face with one of the most despicable acts committed in the days of the Normandy invasion.

CHAPTER TWELVE

PUTOT-EN-BESSIN

After the success the Winnipegs, Carvell amongst them, had with the beach landings and getting to Creully, the battalion would be faced with a battle and enemy that would not be forgotten. [177] The Winnipegs set off from Creully to their final D-Day objective early on the morning of 7 June. C Company led the advance with a platoon from A Company, two section carriers, and one section of 6-pounders.[178] B Company, Carvell in their midst, fresh with reinforcements, stayed close to headquarters during the advancement. They were a little late leaving their positions that morning, leaving at 0615 hours instead of 0600 hours; however, they quickly covered the eight kilometres to Putot. Neither the Winnipegs nor the Regina Rifles had any support during this advance. The Winnipegs met only scattered and ineffective German resistance.[179] They believed that they reached their objective before the Regina Rifles had reached Bretteville l'Orguelleuse and Norrey-en-Bessin.[180] Both regiments quickly began consolidating and digging into their positions.

The Winnipegs were ordered to hold their position and stop any German assault that could threaten the precarious hold the Allies maintained in France.[181] Putot looked like a good, defensible area;[182] however, the Winnipegs would find out how looks can be deceiving. The village, itself, had houses and farms built of Caen stone, making each a potential stronghold against small arms and shrapnel. The Caen-Bayeux railway was an advantage because the Canadian antitank guns would ensure that no tanks would be able to come east. The main problem with trying to defend this area was that there were no good fields of fire between the farm compounds of the village and the rail line to the south. The wheat fields obscured the battlefield. There were also no easy observation, no clear fields of fire, and no real obstacles to vehicle movement on the west of Putot. Seventy years later, when I was on the battlefield of Putot, I could see the inherent difficulties in defense, especially with 1940s technology. Maps showed areas that could provide cover; however, in real life those areas did not provide the cover or obstacles needed. The Winnipegs were also waiting on the British to close the western flank.[183] Putot was a critical point in the bridgehead, and holding the village was essential to preventing these lines of communication (railway) being used by the Germans. Milner also explains that this area was critical to prevent German armour from reaching the beach. As the troops who had landed on said beach had already experienced the horror of German armour, they understood the importance of keeping more away. The Winnipegs had no choice but to ensure that Putot did not fall to the Germans.

Lieutenant Colonel John M. Meldram, commander of the Winnipegs, deployed three companies along the rail line and held one in reserve. He wanted to deploy his three strongest companies to maximize the advantages of Putot defense. Meldram believed that to secure the best view of the terrain to the south, the companies needed to be placed outside the village rather than inside. Major Hodge's A Company, supported by the battalion's 6-pounder antitank guns, covered the rail bridge between Putot and Brouay to the west. Hodge placed one of the platoons north of Brouay, while the other two over looked the bridge.[184] A Company's field of fire was severely restricted and behind them laid the open plain running back towards Sequeville (where the Canadian Scottish was held in reserve). Lieutenant Colonel Meldram knew that he needed to strengthen his flank position until the British showed up.[185] Major Jones's C Company was located along the railway line directly south of Putot. Major Fulton's D Company held the eastern end of the village, facing the rail line where the cutting ended. Captain Gower's rebuilt B Company was designated the battalion reserve and placed in an orchard north of Putot, close to the Battalion headquarters. The orchard contained standing crops which restricted the company's fields of fire to no more than forty to fifty yards.[186] Battalion Headquarters was in farm buildings on the north edge of the village. B Company had received nearly one hundred reinforcements after the initial landings and needed time to reorganize the company.

Lieutenant Colonel Meldram has been highly criticized for his deployment decisions at Putot. Both Stacey and English believe that the battalion was stretched too far, and they were too far forward. Milner echoes Stacey and English belief stating that the Winnipegs were to fight on both a division and a corps boundary.[187] During a patrol, Major Fulton questioned why the stone buildings within the village were not being utilized for defensive positions.[188] This demonstrates that there were some questions as to why they were not using the village for part of their defenses.

By sunset on 7 June, the 7th Brigade was ready for battle. The Battalion's Pioneer Platoon attempted to lay mines in front of A Company south of the railway; however, a German patrol came upon them and forced them to abandon the mines.[189]

Panzers attacked the Winnipegs at around 2100 hours. The attack came on A and C Companies' fronts. A Company was able to repel this attack with only a few casualities. Another batch of reinforcements arrived after this attack and placed in B Company, which was finally up to full strength. The war diary states that enemy snipers kept bothering them throughout the night, but there were no major attacks to the battalion.[190] During the night, the enemy also shot machine guns in hopes of pinpointing the Winnipegs' position. Major Hodge reported hearing enemy tanks off in the far distance at 0400 hours, 8 June. This was the 2nd Battalion of the 26th Panzer Grenadier Regiment of the 12 SS Division, commanded by Lieutenant Colonel Wilhlm Mohnke, making their advance on the Winnipegs.[191] They attacked C Company at around 0430 hours with three tanks; however, the company repelled the attack while suffering two casualties.[192] About 0600 hours, several armoured vehicles accompanied by enemy infantry tried to force their way across the railway bridge opposite of A Company. Major Hodge and his men drove off the small enemy force.[193] Howard Margolian described the Canadians with "their murderous fusillade, coupled with artillery and antitank support, was enough to stop the German advance in its tracks."[194] The Germans quickly learned that the crossing was held in force and would not be easily captured.

The success of this first action was unfortunately short-lived.

The major counterattack by the Germans came at 1000 hours, spotted first by Major Fulton. The tanks rolled in, an estimated twenty to thirty.[195]The German assault came with armour and an artillery barrage as well as an abundance of infantry. The SS youth surged forward, wave after wave, and the Canadians in Putot served them with everything available.[196] D Company had a good field of fire; therefore, they were able to stop this first wave of infantry. This initial fight was not without casualties; four men were killed and twenty had been wounded, nearly a quarter of the company.[197] As the battle wore on, the company received orders to withdraw to defend battalion headquarters.

Against the other Winnipeg positions, the Germans took advantage of the trees and bushes and the steep railway ditch immediately south of Putot to advance onto the Canadian position without detection. The Germans also looked to the west to get around A Company's open flank and cut them off. A Company was in an unfortunate position, being down one platoon and being sited on the main German attack.[198] Major Hodge and his company were attacked by both infantry and twelve to twenty armoured vehicles. They were quickly cut off from their other platoon and their guns were overrun.

Rifleman Hubert recalled that the company could not stop the German forward advance, because the Germans had come between the platoons. If they would have tried to stop the advance, they would have been firing at their own men.[199] The German infantry and armoured vehicles were assisted by numerous snipers inside of Putot and they were able to help bring the Winnipegs under steadily increasing pressure, infiltrating between the company areas.[200] The increased number of snipers in the village made it impossible to get ammunition to the companies, even with a Bren carrier.[201]

Shortly after noon, direct enemy machine gun, mortar, and artillery fire had isolated the forward companies. Elements of A and C Companies were overrun.[202] C Company had been taking heavy machine gun and mortar fire since 0900 hours. They continued to repel the attacks with the use of grenades and smoke; however, the enemy kept coming, seemingly endless waves of infantrymen. Major Jones sent a message to battalion headquarters requesting reinforcements and ammunition.[203] Headquarters was unable to get the reinforcements and ammunition to the company because they too were almost completely overrun. Even in this situation, Major Jones and his men continued to fight and try to meet with other men from the battalion from the other companies.

Rifleman Edward Patey recalled that during the battle that a soldier who was trying to help his wounded companion was riddled with bullets by a nearby German. Patey shot the German, knowing that he would be killed otherwise: "I would have been next on his list, so I shot him...I was fighting for my life and it was not like the cold-blooded SS members."[204] The Winnipegs quickly realized how blood-thirsty the SS youth were when fighting, and they did what they needed to do in order to survive this battle. The soldiers in the Hitler Youth division were seventeen and eighteen-year-olds. They were completely indoctrinated to fight for the Fatherland. Normandy was their first assignment after training.[205] By this point, there was no clear fighting front as more and more Hitler Youth permeated the village. Battalion headquarters had still been reporting that they could handle the situation and were still in control of Putot even though two of their companies had been overrun by the Germans.

Major Hodge and the remnants of A Company, surrounded and short on ammunition, were eventually forced to surrender to the 3rd Battalion, 26th PGR shortly after noon. Meldram had to commit B Company to fight for the village after A Company surrendered. B Company had little communications. Lieutenant Don James, commander of B Company's forward platoon in the wheat fields, had received orders not to fire on any enemy tanks unless his position was given away. German troops, supported by self-propelled guns appeared before James's platoon and quickly overran them.[206] At first, the company was only under artillery and mortar fire before finally coming under full attack. Survivors from A Company made their way to B Company. Most of the company was devoured in the fighting. A, B, and C Companies were completely isolated in the ruins of the village and orchard.[207] Not long after they entered the battle, Captain Gower and about half a dozen of his men surrendered after they were surrounded. He believed he was saving his men's lives by doing this.[208]

Rifleman Johnston was captured with Captain Gower. He described his thoughts on Gower: "I have never met a more courageous officer then Captain Gower and I have always felt honoured to have served with him."[209] Some of the men were able to escape through the tall grass and get back to headquarters. Corporal Wesley Lebarr and a group of thirty or so men had advanced too far and found themselves behind enemy lines. They ran out of ammunition and were forced to surrender. They got rid of anything on themselves that the SS could have used against them before giving themselves up.[210]

D Company was able to extract itself and move back to support the Battalion Headquarters which was also under attack. Headquarters also tried to rescue men from the surrounded companies under the cover of smoke. Only a few survivors made it back to headquarters.[211] Sergeant-Major Charles Belton was fighting with B Company when he was surrounded by the Germans. His carrier was parked close by, so he was able to jump in and escape two German armoured vehicles. He was able to get back to brigade headquarters and brief Brigadier Foster on the situation.[212] By early afternoon, those who were left in the Winnipegs held out around battalion headquarters. D Company, which was almost fully intact, set up a defensive position around headquarters to hold off any more attacks. As soon as the remaining companies had withdrawn from the village, they brought artillery down on the town, but this did not dislodge the enemy who had now surrounded battalion headquarters area by fire.[213]

Later in the afternoon, C Company's commander Major Jones produced a new plan to break back into Putot using two squadrons of tanks from the British Lancers, together with the Canadian infantry. The force was held up by much enemy automatic fire and tanks. The company tried to get in through another route; however, that was held up as well.[214] The attempt failed, but the effort checked German attempts to move beyond Putot to the west.[215] Even with this failed attempt, the Winnipegs still managed to inflict heavy casualties and capture between forty and seventy-five German prisoners. They did not launch a full counterattack to regain the village until later that same evening.

The Canadian Scottish had been listening to the sounds of battles from both the areas of the Winnipegs and the Reginas. To the regiment, it appeared the Germans were fighting two coordinative battles; however, they were fighting two separate battles with little coordination by regimental and divisional headquarters.[216] A few Winnipegs were able to get to the location of D Company of the Can-Scots, and they described the battle taking place. Brigadier Foster was reluctant to commit his reserve unless the situation deemed it. He would only be able to launch one full counterattack and he was not sure whether it would be to Putot or Bretteville-l'Orgueilleuse. Brigadier Foster had warned Lieutenant-Colonel Fred Cabeldu to have the Can-Scots prepare for a possible German breakthrough. At 1830 hours, the orders came in to prepare for a full counterattack on Putot. With the Reginas taking control of their battle and confidently killing the Germans, Foster was able to turn his reserve regiment to Putot. He had a defensive fire plan was in place, but it was complicated because he did not know the exact positions of the remaining Winnipegs.[217]

The Can-Scots had their orders. They needed to capture and hold Putot, as there were no other infantry battalion between Putot and the beaches. The attack went in behind a creeping barrage, and the troops were supported by a squadron of the 1st Hussars. The opposition was heavy, but that did not stop the Can-Scots. After an hour of fighting, reports came that Putot was back in Canadian hands. The German threat was still present after the Can-Scots took Putot; however, the village never went back into German hands. After this battle, the Winnipegs went into reserve. They needed to be reinforced and reorganized after this second set of significant casualties.

This battle was costly. The Winnipegs lost 256 men, including the 150 who were captured. One hundred and five died during or shortly after the battle.[218] The counterattack from the Can-Scots was also costly. They suffered 125 casualties, including forty-five men killed in action.[219] For the Winnipegs, the 150 men who were captured by the Germans, one of whom was George Carvell, would have their lives changed forever. One hundred and ten of the men were turned over to the Feldgendarmerie, the German military police.[220] The forty remaining were escorted to several SS headquarters. Rifleman Carvell was lucky. He was one of the hundred and ten men turned over to the German Army and not kept prisoner by the SS. The 12th SS was known for their brutal treatment of everyone who was not German. Had Carvell not been handed over to the German Army, his final resting place would have been in France and not in New Brunswick. And his death would not have been one that followed military rules of engagement.

Thus began the next chapter in his military career, where he was a prisoner of war.

For Carvell, this was where things came crashing down. He'd survived the landing, seeing his friends mowed down by gunfire, stepping through the blood of his countrymen, fighting boys so young they should have been in the schoolroom, rather than on a battlefield, and being captured. Once he was able wonder what would happen next, the fear set in.[221] Carvell and the other soldiers had not, until this point, had time to think of being afraid when they went into battle. However, once they were standing still as prisoners, the fear caught up with them and the need to survive became their main thoughts.

CHAPTER THIRTEEN

WHAT THESE BATTLES TRULY MEAN

For the Royal Winnipeg Rifles, as well as the other battalions in the 7th and 8th, the Normandy invasion was the first taste of battle for these soldiers who had spent years training in Canada and England. The skills and courage that these men had cannot be understated; however, the 3rd Canadian Infantry Division has faced great criticism for their showing in the invasion. Being on the battlefields and seeing the areas firsthand really changes how you view these battles after the initial beach invasion. It is easy to criticize the soldiers for not meeting their objectives, but some of these objectives were not known at the time of the official history. It was many years later, after the official history was published, that documents were released that the Canadians were there to stop the German panzer attack which could have sent the Allies back to England if they lost. The Canadians held areas and fought the enemy without the help that they were supposed to have (the British did not succeed in their objective, which led the Winnipegs to be overrun). Reinforcement men came into units that just lost hundreds of their comrades and they were expected to just start fighting as a unit, even though most of these units were together training for the last four years. The men were in impossible situations but they still showed more bravery than what could have been asked.

Stacey questioned why more was not achieved during that first day of the beach landings.[222] He asserted that the Canadians should have been able to obtain their D-Day objectives, but the training of the Canadians was not to the calibre of the Germans. This was the first time that the division saw combat. Training gave them so much, but real experience became their new teacher and they accomplished much more than they are given credit for. Copp disagrees with Stacey's assessment of the Canadians and counters the argument. He maintains that the Canadian Army has been underestimated and the Germans have been exaggerated.[223] Milner agrees with Copp's assessment and argues that if it was not for the 3rd Canadian Infantry Division and their abilities to take the beach and hold the area that the continued invasion would have failed. The men suffered and sacrificed terribly on the beach landings, but they continued to fight to achieve their objectives. Carvell did not stop fighting when faced with this impossible task; none of the men did.

The Battle of Putot is an important battle in the Winnipegs history and in my family's history. This battle and the fighting abilities of the Winnipegs during the battle have faced criticism in the Normandy narrative. When I stood at the rail lines that the men were supposed to defend and looked out to the area, I could not understand why they were criticized so much. The Winnipegs had more indefinable land with fewer men than they needed and against an enemy who was out for blood. Stacey describes the 8 June battles, Putot and Bretteville, as a series of violent local counter attacks. This downplays the battles and what the Winnipegs achieved during those first few days after the invasion. They were much more than just local counter attacks; these were the difference of liberating France and failing. He quickly points out the superb abilities of the Canadian Scottish and how they were able to take back the village within an hour.[224] Stacey was harsh in his treatment of the training of the reinforcement units and the ability of their men to actually fight once they were within the regular regiments. The Winnipegs had lost so many men in the initial beach landings that the reinforcement soldiers had to be quickly absorbed into the regiment and ready for battle. Some of these men were only with the battalion for a day before seeing action. Brigadier Foster stated that the Winnipegs were overrun "chiefly owing to the fact that one assault company had been practically obliterated on the beach and the gaps in its ranks had had to be replaced by reinforcements of all sorts, some not even infantry."[225] There had been no time to re-organize the company.

English is especially hard on the Winnipegs and their performance at Putot. He argues that the Winnipegs were put to flight in this battle and uses this battle to highlight the failings of the Canadian Army in Normandy. He states that three German companies put three Canadian companies to flight.[226] Milner points out that three under strength and—in some cases—recently rebuilt assault companies were vastly outnumbered by the three over-strength companies of the 12th SS that attacked. While the Winnipegs companies had a national strength of 119 of all ranks, the SS companies numbered 200 or more.[227] So the Winnipegs were significantly outnumbered. Mark Zuehike is critical of the reinforcements that were placed in B Company. He states that he believed that a good number of the men were inadequately trained.[228] The reinforcement units had the same training; they were forced to learn how to fight in a unit that was tight knit and grieving for the many comrades who just died. They were in a difficult situation but did their best against all odds.

I agree with Both Bechthold and Milner opposition of English's argument. Bechthold argues that the Winnipegs did not collapse under the attack of the 12th SS Panzer Division; rather, held on until Brigadier Foster could organize a well-coordinated counterattack to recapture Putot.[229] He also argues against English in that there were more than just three German companies that attacked the Winnipegs. The Germans also had a fourth heavy weapons company with the infantry.[230] A Winnipeg collapse would also have had dire consequences for the Reginas' position in Bretteville-Norrey to the east. The battle was not a victory for the Winnipegs; however, they were not put to flight. Reid states that Putot was a tactical defeat for the Winnipegs; however, it was a strategic victory because they stalled the enemy's advance.[231] Milner agrees with Bechthold's argument and that they stayed fighting. They held the village to deny the Germans the possibility of pushing through to the English Channel. The Canadian's objective on 7 and 8 June was to deny a German panzer advance and they achieved this. Carvell was proud of what he and the Winnipegs accomplished on D-Day, and he knew they fought hard in Putot even with the causalities. They accomplished their objective of holding the Germans back.

Chapter Fourteen

The Geneva Convention and the Treatment of POWs

No soldier ever believes that he or she will be captured by the enemy. Training focuses on staying alive during battle and fighting. Soldiers were trained on how to treat prisoners of war (POWs), but were given little information about what to do if they were captured. For George Carvell, becoming a prisoner of war was unexpected and put his survival in the hands of the enemy. Nothing could have prepared him for what he would endure in the next eleven months as a POW.

Guilt often riddled the prisoners. They blamed themselves for getting captured and being unable to continue to fight. They'd been trained for years that their purpose was to fight. Every day, they drilled and practiced and had it shouted at them from their superiors that they were there because they had a job to do. They had to *fight!* The purpose of a soldier is to fight a battle. They drilled and practiced until their bodies could perform the necessary tasks simply by instinct. But being captured stopped that cold, leaving them in a situation that they had no training for and no guidance on how to react.. However, prisoners from the Normandy campaign like those from the Dieppe Raid and Hong Kong all had one thing in common: they worked to survive at all costs and to do whatever they could to assist in the war effort against the enemy.

The Second World War stands out in terms of scale and range of treatment exhibited by captor states. Approximately 35 million soldiers (both Allied and Axis) spent time in enemy hands through the war.[232] The treatment given to the POWs, nonetheless, depended on the nationality of both captive and captor and the period of the war. The treatment could range from the strict adherence to the terms of the Geneva Convention to brutality severe enough to claim approximately 5 million lives.[233] The Geneva Convention of 1929, through the League of Nations, provided a detail list of the rights of prisoners and the responsibilities of the captors. The convention supplemented the Hague Convention of 1907, which had attempted to regulate the means of war. The Geneva Convention of 1929 was widely accepted. Germany signed the original Convention and ratified it in 1934. Japan, on the other hand, only signed but did not ratify it. All the Western Allies signed and ratified the Convention. Canada signed in 1930 and ratified it in 1933.

One of the most important rights of a prisoner was in Article 2 of the Convention which states that prisoners must, at all times, "be humanely treated and protected, particularly against acts of violence, from insults and public curiosity."[234] This would help to shelter the prisoners from any undue harm at the hands of their captors. Article 5 dictated what information was required of soldiers who were captured and interrogated by the enemy. Soldiers were obligated to state their name, rank, and regimental number , but that was it. Prisoners who refused to offer more information were not to be threatened, insulted, or exposed to unpleasantness.[235] Canadian soldiers learned this during their years of training in Britain. The Convention also outlined how prisoner of war camps were to operate, the sort of work prisoners were allowed to do, contact with the outside world, and penal laws used in the camps. This convention was erected after the tragedies of the First World War in hopes that if another war broke out, that inevitable result of armed conflict (POWs)would be treated with humanity.

These articles would only work, however, if the captors abided by them. Japan did not ratify them, so it was under no legal obligations to follow them.[236] Germany had signed and ratified the Geneva Convention and so ought to have abided by them. However, the Germans did not follow all responsibilities to which they had agreed.[237] As the war continued, the treatment deteriorated due to the lack of supplies and lack of care for the well-being for the prisoners.

CHAPTER FIFTEEN

BEING A POW: NORMANDY, DIEPPE AND HONG KONG

Treatment of prisoners varied depending on the camp, the prisoner's rank, the prisoner's nationality, and other contributing factors. The Germans treated the Western Allies (including Canadians) far better than they did Eastern European soldiers. The individual prisoner's race was placed into the context of the Nazi racial hierarchy. Anglo-Saxons, Germanic people, and Greeks were better respected than those of Gallic descent and Slavs. Western Jews in uniform were generally left untouched when captured because the secrecy of the Final Solution could not be achieved if they were harmed.[238] If the Westerns Jews in uniform were murdered in the prison camps it would compromise the Final Solution. Hitler wanted that to be kept from the Allies for as long as possible. When mistreatment was discovered, the Allies issued warnings that those responsible would be put on trial after the war for war crimes. The fear of personal indictment and fear of retaliation were generally enough for the Germans to ensure the proper treatment of POWs.

The Japanese did not feel the same fears, and Canadians captured in Hong Kong experienced horrors that those who were captured in Europe would not have to endure. There has been much discussion of why the Japanese treated their prisoners with such brutality. S. P. MacKenzie argues that the extreme, brutal treatment was in part based on the Japanese military tradition that demanded absolute sacrifice and deemed surrender an unbearable dishonour. He also argues that the treatment stemmed from a growing xenophobic nationalism in Japan that was caused by the stress of the interwar years.[239] The actual spirit of the Japanese warrior code involves fair and enlightened treatment for captured enemy forces. However, with the emphasis of surrender as shameful and the brutality within the wartime Japanese military ideology did not bode well for humane treatment of Allied POWs.[240]

A. Hamish Ion argues that the mistreatment of the Canadians and Allied POWs was more the product of the chaos of war than a deliberate policy.[241] The Japanese were not equipped to handle the number of POWs who came into their custody at the beginning of the war. Their resources were stretched thin, and they simply did not know what to do with all the prisoners. Ion also argues that since there was no deliberate policy of treatment, it was individuals (camp commanders, guards, doctors, etc) who were responsible for the type of treatment that the POWs received.

The Canadian government never wanted to send troops to Hong Kong, because Hong Kong was a British Crown colony, and Canada was hesitant to send soldiers to protect British imperialism. However, after pressure from Britain, Canada sent two battalions for garrison duty in late 1941.[242] The Royal Rifles of Canada and the Winnipeg Grenadiers were chosen for this post.[243] The Canadian soldiers were a part of a largely British and Indian garrison. They were told that the Japanese were ill equipped, unused to night fighting, and only totalled about 5000 men, therefore, they would not be a threat to the men. The Japanese attacked the Canadian position on 18 December 1941. By Christmas, the Canadians and British had surrendered and for almost the next four years, the survivors of this surrender had to survive being POWs in a nation that rejected the Geneva Convention and viewed soldiers who surrendered as cowards.[244]

The Canadians captured in Hong Kong endured unspeakable horrors that no other Canadian POWs experienced.

Life in the Japanese POW camps was very different from anything the Canadians had witnessed, no matter where they had gone throughout the course of the war. Flight Lieutenant Robert Wyse of Newcastle, New Brunswick, was with the Royal Air Force when he was captured by the Japanese in March 1942.

He kept a detailed diary of his experiences in the Japanese camps and the horrors that he witnessed.[245] In his first camp, Malang Prison Camp, the prisoners lived in terrible conditions and had little to no food. They quickly found the biggest killers of the prisoners were malnutrition and disease.[246] About 24.8 percent of the British and 41.6 percent of the American prisoners lost their lives from disease, malnutrition, overwork, or deliberate murder.[247] The camp had no running water and no amenities for the men. They used a small stream close to the camp for water until it dried out and they tried to get the men to use the bathroom away from the living quarters. However, most did not go far, which made the camp unbearable. Due to the lack of water and improper toilet facilities, dysentery[248] and scabies spread through the camp. These diseases could have easily been cured had the treatment been more available.

The Western prisoners had a hard time adjusting to the new diet as well. Most of the meals consisted of rice and little else. Sometimes they would be given stew and bread with tea. The men needed fruits and vegetable to maintain their health. Officers were able to buy some fruits and vegetables once they started receiving their pay. They created a black market, giving more prisoners the ability to obtain extra food. At times, Wyse noticed how selfish the officers were becoming after being in the camps for over a year. Some officers would not give any of their extra food to the men who needed it; they kept everything for themselves.[249] The lack of vitamins in the food caused numerous illnesses such as beriberi, pellagra, temporary blindness, and electric feet.[250] These illnesses could have been easily cured with the proper nutrition.

Even with the lack of food, the Canadians were forced into doing back-breaking labour for the Japanese. The Japanese expected the Japanese people to work for the war effort, so they expected that POWs should be made to engage in forced labour even when the Convention explicitly states that POWs are not to do any labour to help the war effort.[251] The general principle that the Japanese adhered to for their prisoners was that the privates worked, NCOs supervised, and officers did not have to work. There were exceptions made to these principles, and many officers were forced to do brutally heavy work along with their men.[252]

The working day for the prisoners was between fourteen and sixteen hours long. Medical officers were an exception to this principle. They all worked, and the Japanese used them for some humanitarian intent. Some officers wished that they could get work for exercise and mental stimulation. The men also tried smuggling goods back to the camp from working, but that quickly stopped when they got caught. Wyse described how they were forced to work on aerodomes to extend the runways, filling in bomb holes and drainage ditches, and shifting bombs, oil, and petrol. [253] This back-breaking work was compounded by the lack of food and the rampant illness. The men were forced to work even when they were sick and had skin sores. The Japanese wanted 750 men from Wyse's camp, to work every day. If that number of men did not show up, they cut food rations. For the type of labour they were being forced to do, the food rations were not enough to sustain the men. For sixteen-hour work days, they were given a breakfast of rice, lunch of a bun, and supper was more rice. The lack of food eventually led to many prisoners to being unable to work because of illness. Even Wyse spent a significant amount of time in the hospital due to the numerous maladies that he contracted while in the camp. They were treated as slave labourers, obtaining little pay for their work, and they were subjected to constant beatings.

While the work itself was brutal, the treatment that the prisoners endured at the work sites was appalling. The guards harassed them constantly and beat them ceaselessly. One POW was not working hard enough, and the guard hit him across the head with his rifle butt and knocked him down. When the prisoner got up, he took a swing at the guard and another guard stabbed him in the stomach with a bayonet.[254] The prisoner survived the brutal punishment. Punishments took place without legal niceties.[255]

Punishments were common in the camps for everything. Japanese disciplinary code varied from harsh to the intolerable depending on the outlook of individual camp guards and commandants.[256] The Japanese guards gave out daily beatings for not saluting an officer, not getting to roll call on time, for frying rice, and for stealing.[257] Punishments for trying to escape were significantly worse than anything the Canadians had witnessed anywhere else.

The Japanese implemented measures to ensure that the prisoners would not attempt escape. They required all men to sign a contract stating that they would not attempt escape and if they did they would be executed for breaking their promise.[258] The prisoners who were not executed were turned over to the Kemeitai (military secret police). If one was caught trying to escape, they were made an example of to deter others from trying to do the same. The whole camp also suffered when an escape was attempted. Often, they were forced to parade outside most of the night then had to get up for work the next morning.[259] Wyse described an incident where two men tried to escape so they could call their wives who lived in the town by the camp. The men were tied to trees by wire and were tortured, receiving punishment every hour and food only once a day.[260] Sometimes, this torture took place in bamboo cages set in view of the camp. Some escapees were beaten with baseball bats and barbed wire in front of everyone. These punishments deterred many of the prisoners from attempting to escape.

The Western soldiers saw attempting escape as both desirable and military correct. Even though it was not considered shameful to be captured (if one had fought as valiantly as possible before surrendering), POWs from Western nations did face their military's expectations that they would attempt to escape. It was part of their duty. However, while their military code may have prompted escape attempts, most prisoners of the Japanese simply ignored the whole idea and set themselves to the task of surviving. Escaping was also difficult for the Canadians from a logistical perspective.[261] In Europe, one could possibly pass oneself off as German, at least visually. There were resistance networks. However, an Anglo-Saxon Canadian could not make himself look Japanese. Few spoke the language, and there were no resistance networks available to help the Allied cause.

A scholar can easily paint a picture of brutality when describing the Hong Kong camps; however, not everything that occurred in the camps was negative. The prisoners did get a reprieve from the horrors in numerous ways. Those strong enough to participate played sports. The camp guards organized ball games between the prisoners. When the food supply increased, more men would play. Officers often played the most sports because they had more access to other food and more energy to play. Cricket, field hockey, and soccer were all popular in the camps until the equipment wore out. Once that occurred, the games ended since it was almost impossible to get equipment replaced.

Sports helped some with morale; however, the prisoners found other ways to keep with spirits up and occupy their free time. Many of the Canadians who had instruments with them before they were captured were able to bring them to the camps. While some traded their instruments for extra rations, many continued playing there. Bands and orchestras sprung up, and the prisoners thoroughly enjoyed the concerts. It helped to raise morale among the soldiers, perhaps even more so than the sports. Reading was also a popular activity among the men. Most camps managed to establish a rudimentary library allowing men who were too sick to work to now use books to pass the hours. Some even started writing their own novels to occupy their time. Wyse described starting to write a novel to keep himself amused.[262] Men had to find any way to keep them going on a daily basis. They played card games and board games. Bridge was the most played card game within the camps, and checkers and chess were common as well.

Receiving mail boosted morale most of all. Mail did not come often as the men would have liked. Wyse was not able to write a letter home until almost a year after he had been captured.[263] Squad. Leader L. J. Birchall was captured in 1942. He was allowed to write a few postcards home while in the camps in Japan.[264] Each postcard was similar in nature stating that he was well, that he has not heard anything from his wife, and that he hoped she would remember him always.[265] He was allowed to write a few two-page letters to his wife. Birchall never received any letters from her, but did receive a few from his parents. Mail was not always reliable because the Japanese often destroyed the letters before they were ever mailed. Some prisoners were able to make radio broadcasts to their families. Birchill's wife received a telegram with the transcript of a radio broadcast that her husband gave on 29 July 1944.[266] Even with the restrictions and knowing that the letters did not always get sent, the prisoners still wrote home and anxiously waited for a response. The hope for a response was often what kept the men going in the camps.

The Germans did not treat Canadians POWs with the same brutality that the Japanese did. There were two major waves of Canadian POWs captured in France in the Second World War. The first were taken in 1942, in the aftermath of the Dieppe Raid. The second wave were captured in 1944, in the days after the cross-channel invasion on the French coastline of Normandy. The Dieppe and Normandy POWs had very similar experiences. For the nearly 2000 Canadians captured in Dieppe, becoming a prisoner left them feeling guilty that they would no longer be able to continue fighting the enemy. The men who were capture at Puys (Blue Beach) and Pourville (Green Beach) were marched in the towns before being marched into Dieppe with the rest of the Canadians.

Jack A Poolton, of the Royal Regiment of Canada, surrendered on Puys with more than two hundred of his regiment. He stated in his memoir that, "you can train a soldier to fight and you can train a soldier to accept death, but there is no way to prepare a soldier to be taken prisoner."[267] He describes the feelings of humiliation and that only men who have been prisoners would understand these feelings. These were common emotions among all POWs regardless of where they were captured, and they never disappeared even after liberation. To my knowledge, George Carvell never spoke of feelings of guilt or humiliation for being captured. He spoke very little about his time as a POW to our family at all.

At Dieppe, the Germans gave the wounded first aid and moved them to the hospital,[268] while they paraded those who were able to walk through the city. They required some to march to holding camps before moving them to more permanent camps. The marches would be similar to those of the Normandy POWs. The Germans provided no food. The French tried to help the soldiers by giving them food, water, and clothing along the way. The train served as a main source of transportation for Dieppe prisoners. Poolton ended up in a boxcar with fifty other men. These conditions were even worse than what Carvell would endure two years later. The men were only able to stand or squat in the area; there was no room to lie down to rest or sleep. Food was also hard to come by. They were given a round loaf of black bread that needed to last at least five days.[269] The conditions on the train deteriorated as the time progressed. The air turned foul within the cars from the improper toilet facilities (they had only a pail). The wounded men's injuries became infected and riddled with maggots. The cars were also filled with bugs.

These were indeed appalling conditions that the men had to endure while travelling to the camps. However, there was always the pastime of escape. As I mentioned earlier, the military codes of the Western Allied countries expected captured soldiers to make all reasonable efforts to escape. In this case, many men concluded that this stretch of travel would be the easiest time to actually get away from their captors. Poolton planned his escape while on the train; however, fate stepped in and he was not able to.[270] The Germans told all the prisoners that if anyone escaped off the train, ten men would be shot. This did not leave Poolton's mind while he was trying to find a way to escape. There was an opening on the train car that Poolton was on. Other soldiers escaped through this opening; however, Poolton was stopped by a Canadian sergeant who ordered him not to leave the car.[271] Escaping while on the train was also popular during the Normandy POW transfers.

The Dieppe POWs were placed in numerous camps in Germany. Poolton and most other members from the Royal Regiment of Canada were sent to Stalag VIIIB.[272] Others ended up in Stalag Luft III at Sagan in Silesia and Oflag VIIB Eichstätt. Stalag VIIIB was located at Lamsdorf, near the Lower Silesia city of Oppeln.

The camp was known colloquially as Hell Camp. It had been used as a prison camp during the First World War, and it was resurrected for the Second. The camp was quite large, which resulted in the POWs having little contact with the German authorities. Conditions were harsh. There was little food when the prisoners arrived in the camp, no utensils, and very few blankets.[273] The camp was often overcrowded and the men lived in poor conditions.

Through conditions were not comfortable, they were not as horrific as those that the Canadians captured in Hong Kong faced. Diseases did not run through the camps at the extent that they did in the Japanese camps. The sick did receive medical treatment. The Red Cross packages helped to supplement the diet and provide the needed medical supplies for the sick.[274] Robert Prouse recalled that the Red Cross parcels saved them from starving. They were supposed to arrive every week; however, sometimes the Germans would keep the parcels for themselves instead of giving them to the prisoners.[275] Next of kin could send parcels to the POWs, but they could not contain food aside from chocolate. The parcels often contained clothing, toiletries, and recreational material.[276]

One of the most controversial aspects of the Dieppe POWs experience was the shackling of the prisoners. Under the Geneva Convention, reprisals against prisoners were prohibited regardless of how big or small they were. The controversy started after the Dieppe Raid when reports surfaced that the British had tied up some of the German prisoners that they captured. In the military plan for the raid, against the wishes of the Canadian Division commander, it was recommended that prisoners be bound to prevent the destruction of their documents.[277] This was common practice of the British Special Service Brigade to tie prisoners taken during a raid.[278] This plan might have remained a secret were it not for the capture of a copy of the plan after the surrender of Canadian troops at Dieppe. There were also rumors that the shackling was in retaliation for German prisoners who were found shot with their hands tied behind their backs.[279] Whatever the real reason, the German government decided to shackle their prisoners, including the Canadians.

On 8 October 1942, German soldiers used rope to tie Poolton and the other Royal Regiment of Canada members at Stalag VIIIB in groups of ten. The groups had to do everything together, which was inconvenient for everyone involved. The use of ropes only lasted for eight weeks before shackles appeared at the camps. The shackles proved to be less of a challenge, as the POWs learned to remove the shackles with keys from sardine cans.[280] The men would try confusing the Germans during the shackling process by removing the shackles, then going back in line to be bound again. One of the downsides to the shackles was that the men often got sores on their wrists. In the Oflag VIIB Eichstatt camp, the binding of all Canadians only lasted for three days before camp officials decided that they would select twenty men to be shackled each day.[281]

Not all Germans agreed with the shackling of the prisoners. According to Vance, while the German government pushed for the binding, the German soldiers thought it was distasteful.[282] They were embarrassed by committing such an act. The guards knew it was against military protocol and beneath their dignity as citizen soldiers. The prisoners also did not make the process easy for the guards. The shackling often took most of the day, instead of the hour it should have. This situation escalated when the British government decided to shackle more German prisoners. Retaliation continued between the countries, and the Canadian government reluctantly supported the British. The British and Canadian governments finally announced on 10 December that the German POWs would be unshackled. The Germans did not perceive this announcement as enough of a guarantee that shackling would not continue; therefore, they continued to shackle Allied POWs. They wanted the Allies to put a policy in place that would ensure that prisoners would not be shackled.[283]

Poolton described being shackled for 410 days, with the shackles being on from 0600 to 2000 hours each day. Being in shackles for such long periods of time did put quite the damper on the men's favourite pastime of trying to escape. However, once the shackling discontinued, the men escalated their escape attempts again.

Many prisoners viewed it as their duty to attempt escape by any means necessary. Each soldier had his own reasons, including such things as a thirst for adventure, returning to loved ones, and their military duty to escape.[284] The Dieppe POWs found numerous methods to escape from the trains and camps. Tunnels and disguises were both very popular means of trying to get out. It was significantly easier to escape from the German camps than from the Japanese ones due to the relative ease of disguising oneself (as the captors and the captives were generally the same race) and the proximity of resistance networks and available help. Punishments for escaping varied among the camps.

While the POWs in Germany were technically under the protection of the Geneva Convention, some escapees were more harshly punished for their attempts. The Germans had numerous problems trying to prevent escape from Stalag Luft III. There were two major escapes at this camp, one in 1943 and the other 1944. The 1944 escape was known as the "Great Escape" as seventy-six men managed to get out of the camp. Fifty of the men were recaptured and executed as a deterrent for others.[285] These POWs were from the air force, but their escape affected the Dieppe POWs punishment for escape attempts. This was an example of the extreme punishments that the Germans imposed on the men who attempted escape. Poolton escaped a couple of times. Each time, he was recaptured and sentenced to solitary confinement,[286] the norm for punishment after an escape attempt.

Not every prisoner desired escape. Some were so hungry, exhausted, and demoralized or disoriented that their thoughts turned instead to food and rest. For them, the relative comforts of a permanent POW camp seemed much more appealing than the uncertainty and privations of escape and flight.[287]

For those who decided to stay in the camps, they tried their best to make life as enjoyable as possible. Prouse claimed that the main reason prisoners were able to endure the camps was because of the comradeship and unselfishness of most prisoners.[288] Similar to those in Japanese camps, prisoners in German camps found activities and games to pass the time. The Normandy POWs took up many of the same activities. However, their activities were generally limited because they moved between camps so often, whereas the Dieppe soldiers spent significantly more time in the camps. Poker and bridge were popular card games, using cigarettes for betting and in auctions. The camp leaders organized plays for the men. Musicians were able to obtain instruments and performed concerts on Saturday nights.[289] If the camps were not under punishment, they were often allowed to hold boxing matches. The men were able to play many sports. Canadian cities sent sporting equipment to the prisoners through the Red Cross. One of the camps received hockey equipment from Calgary.[290] These little touches of home helped to keep up the morale of the soldiers.

Chapter Sixteen

Murders by the 12th SS Panzer Division

Though the Geneva Convention was supposed to ensure the safety and proper treatment of the prisoners of war, however, George Carvell quickly discovered that was not always the case. He came a hairsbreadth away from falling victim to one of the most egregious lapses of the rules of engagement in the Normandy campaign.

Carvell's captured came at the hand of the 2nd Battalion of the 26th Panzer Grenadier Regiment on 8 June 1944. He was one of the more than one hundred Canadians who were taken prisoner that day. His group was turned over to the Feldgendarmerie (German Army) for transport to the rear. They arrived at SS Lieutenant Colonel Wilhelm Mohnke's regimental command post in Le Haut de Bosq later that afternoon.[291]

When interviewed for an article in 1994, George Carvell recalled that he was with a group of twenty other prisoners. They waited, huddled together, for what would happen next as the rumours began to circulate. Canadians were being executed by Germans, people were saying. They just lined them up and shot them. Was that the gunfire they had been hearing? Was that about to happen to them?

None of them would hear the full story until after the war.

Against the Geneva Convention, the 12th SS Panzer Division would, on 7 and 8 June, choose to commit murder. Perhaps it is odd to think about there being a concept such as murder between enemies in an armed conflict. But that is part of what rules of engagement and the Geneva Convention are about. It is only legal to kill your enemies under certain conditions. If that enemy has surrendered to you, you are no longer permitted to kill him or her. They are now prisoners and must be treated under the protection of the Geneva Convention. If you choose to ignore this protection, it's murder.

I had the privilege of visiting some of the sites of these murders during a battlefield study tour that I went on. This study tour was for Canadian students to walk the grounds of the First and Second World War battles to gain a better understanding of the battles and the role of Canada in them. The Normandy battles were especially important for myself, including seeing the place where my Uncle George came close to being murdered. I got to know some of the soldiers who were as lucky as my uncle to survive. It was important for me to remember these men who were murdered.

There were forty remaining prisoners who were marched to their headquarters which was located on the farm of George Moulin in Le Mesnil-Patry. The SS troops distributed water and first aid supplies to the wounded. The prisoners were placed the Moulin's barn.[292] These men were retained for interrogation before being handed over to the Feldgendarmerie. These men were never handed over to the Feldgendarmerie. Instead they waited two more days before they met their untimely end.

Just two miles west of where the others were captured and being held, there was another group of prisoners, twenty-four Winnipegs and two British, who were marched in the direction of the village of Pavie, near where Lieutenant-Colonel Gerhard Bremer's 12th SS Reconnaissance Battalion had its headquarters.

Major Hodge, Commander of A Company, thirteen members of his company's 9th Platoon, including the Meakin brothers from Birnie, Manitoba, eight men from 7th and 8th Platoons, and two reinforcements from Queen's Own Rifles (QOR) ended up in the custody of Bremer's men.[293] Germans took the Allied troops taken to the Château d'Audrieux, in Pavie to be interrogated. The prisoners were searched as soon as they arrived, their documents were taken, and all their personal effects were thrown away.[294] After the searches, the interrogations began.

Major Hodge, Lance Corporal Austin Fuller (RWR), and Private Frederick Smith (QOR) were the first ones to be interrogated. Since Bremer was fluent in English, he did most of the questioning. Hodge revealed nothing more than his name, rank, and military identification number. Bremer had no luck with retrieving any information from the other two soldiers. Getting nowhere with the interrogation, Bremer resorted to a rather archaic and ungentle-manly method of dealing with enemy prisoners.

He ordered them to be shot.

SS Sergeant Stunn carried out Bremer's orders, marching the men out to the edge of a wooded area just outside of the Château. Fuller, Smith, and Hodge quickly realized what was going to happen, but they made no desperate attempts to escape, nor any pleas for mercy.[295] From all accounts, these men walked to their deaths with pride and dignity, even though they must have known that what was about to happen was against the rules of warfare that they had been told their enemy would follow. Stunn forced the three Canadians to turn their backs. The executioners shot Hodge first, hitting his shoulder and then his head. Fuller and Smith turned around just before the shots fired, confronting their murderers.

They both died quickly.

As the first group fell under their murderers' bullets, the next set of prisoners went into interrogation. Again, Bremer received no information, and he gave another order of execution. Due to the confrontations from Fuller and Smith during the first execution, Bremer ordered for the next group to be shot in the head. The three men were all shot at point-blank range and died instantly from the massive head wounds. Bremer quickly realized that interrogating the men three at a time and then shooting them would take all day. Therefore, he sent the remaining thirteen Winnipegs (the Meakin brothers among them) to the orchard to be killed. The SS troops had rifles, the NCOs had machine guns, and officers had their side arms ready to fire. The men were lined in a row facing them when the Germans opened fire. The eldest

Meakin brother, George jumped in front of the younger, Frank, in a desperate attempt to take the bullets meant for him and perhaps save his life. Unfortunately, his sacrifice was in vain, as Frank was shot in the head just after.[296]

I spent time reading George Meakin's service file and letters to his mother during my research for the battlefield's study tour. I presented a biography of him at his grave site in Beny-sur-Mer cemetery. It was a sobering moment standing at his grave, reading about his final moments and the last letter he wrote his mother:

This may be the last chance I get to write before the big day, so if you don't hear from me for a while, please try not and not worry. We will be ok. And no what happens, we are all coming back and all in one piece. I am as always your most loving son and brother. George.[297]

Three weeks later, the British found the bodies of the other five Canadians and two British POWs who were the original group of twenty-six. They bodies were close to where the first two groups of prisoners were murdered.

Figure 8: George Meakin's grave at Beny-sur-Mer, 2014
Author's personal collection.

Figure 9: Frank Meakin's grave at Beny-sur-Mer, 2014
Author's personal collection.

Sergeant-Major Charles Belton, B Company RWR, was in the group that found Major Hodge and his murdered men. Belton recalled that Hodge was unrecognizable, as his face had been shot away. The only way he was able to identify Hodge was from a gold bracelet with his name and regimental number on it that his mother had given him.[298] One of Belton's cousins was murdered there, as well as many other friends. He was previously in A Company before getting his promotion; therefore, he was friends with all the murdered men he found. Belton stated that these murders "went against the rules of war, but some parts of the Second World War didn't have any rules."[299]

The murders that took place at the Château d'Audrieux were not an isolated event. During the Battle of Authie and Buron on 7 June 1944, a small group of Canadians from the 9th Brigade (Highland Light Infantry, the Stormont Dundas and Glengarry Highlanders, North Nova Scotia Highlanders and 27th Canadian Armoured Regiment—the Sherbrooke Fusilier Regiment) were taken prisoner and brought to the headquarters of SS Standartenführer Kurt Meyer at the Abbaye d'Ardenne.[300] Twelve North Novas and six Sherbrookes were brought to the abbaye.

Once at the abbaye, the SS searched the men and took papers and personal items from them. The Germans asked for volunteers from the Canadians; however, no one wanted to volunteer until they knew for what they were volunteering for. The Germans decided to pick ten men: Corporal Joseph MacIntyre, Privates Ivan Crown, Charles Doucette, James Moss, Lieutenant Thomas Windsor, Troopers James Bolt, George Gill, Thomas Henry, Roger Lockhead, and Harold Philip.[301] The Germans also added Hollis McKeil, who was severely wounded, to the group of men, who were immediately taken to the chateau for interrogation.

The Canadians were brought to the abbaye gardens one at a time to be interrogated. They knew that they only had to supply the enemy with their name, rank, and ID number under the Geneva Convention. The Germans continued to ask for more information; however, the Canadians refused to give them any.

The first interrogation abruptly and brutally ended with the Germans killing him with crushing blows to the head.[302] The Germans did this with six of the Canadians before they got tired of beating their prisoners to death. Lieutenant Windsor and the four remaining men would all be interrogated, and when they did not give the answers that the Germans were looking for, were shot in the head.[303]

The following day, 8 June, seven more Canadian prisoners would meet the same fate and were shot after their interrogations did not result in information. In total, eighteen men were shot in the gardens of the abbaye between 7 and 8 June. Two more would meet a similar fate days later.[304] The Battle of Authie resulted in fifty-five Canadians being murdered at the hands of the 12th SS Panzer Division. While all of the murders were horrendous, the murders at the abbaye were cold, calculated, and systematic.[305] It was during this time that the 12th SS became known as the "murder division."

The bodies of these men were not discovered until after the war. The owners (Mr. and Mrs. Vico) of the abbaye came back after the war and had always had a beautiful garden just off of the courtyard. When they arrived, they saw that their garden was not growing where it should. As they sifted the garden beds, they started to uncover the bodies of the Canadians. They left markers at the areas where they found bodies, so the authorities could dig them up, identify them, and notify their families.

I have been in that garden at the abbaye. It is a very humbling and sobering place to be. It is beautiful, with flowers and trees hiding a precious memorial to the men who were murdered there. You have to move through the space and look for it. This act of moving into the garden to see the pictures of the men on the wall of the building just draws you into the memorial and the meaning of the garden. For me, one of the hardest moments about seeing the men's photographs on the wall was seeing Lieutenant Windsor. He was a relative to my professor Dr. Windsor, and knowing the connection, made the moment even more sobering. The memorial is simple, but it evokes powerful emotions about what happened there. I participated in a ceremony for the 70th anniversary of the murders and place a maple leaf on the memorial for soldiers.

Figure 10: The Abbaye d'Ardenne, 2014. Author's personal collection.

Figure 11: Memorial to the Canadians who were murdered in the garden, 2014. Author's personal collection.

One hundred and fifty-six Canadians were murdered during the first ten days of the Normandy Invasion. Some of these murders took place when soldiers were trying to surrender[306], the wounded in the battles were often murdered instead of given medical treatment and those on forced marches to the POW camps had to contend with being mowed down by the Germans passing by in vehicles and airplanes. Most of these men were murdered for the simple fact they would not give information to the enemy, others were murdered just because they were trying to liberate the French from the Nazis. Howard Margolian ended his book *Conduct Unbecoming* with a powerful tribute to the fallen Canadians: the victims of the Normandy massacres told us something about their character, about what was in their hearts. By their acts of decency, in the shadow of their own deaths, they preserved for all time that which their killers had tried to erase with cowardly murders and unmarked graves—their essential humanity.[307]

Not all the soldiers who ended up at the abbaye after capture were murdered. While the soldiers in the garden were being murdered, hundreds of other POWs, who were captured on 7 June, were in the courtyard of the abbaye. They remained there until they could be moved to a POW camp. Major Jack M. Veness, Major Jack L. Fairweather, and Major Don Learment (North Novas) marched to the Abbaye before moving to a POW camp.[308]

All of these atrocities occurred at the hands of the 12th SS (Hitler Youth). Carvell, Vaness, Fairweather, and Learment were all taken prisoner by the SS, but their time with the SS was mercifully short. The German Army treated their prisoners differently than the SS did.

So there was my great-great uncle, George Carvel, sitting at SS Lieutenant Colonel Wilhelm Mohnke's regimental command post in Le Haut de Bosq waiting to know his fate. At twenty-one years old, he survived days of continual gunfire, watching his friends fall all around him, now he was at the mercy of the enemy, having absolutely no control over what happens next. He could only hope and pray that he would not meet the same fate of the men who had already been shot. Luck was on Carvell's side, as a German soldier of higher rank ended the executions before they could get to Carvell's group:

We had heard the day before that the Germans had lined up and shot 27 prisoners and we were terrified when they lined us up. To add to our fears, a Ukrainian among us translated the German language and said we were going to be shot. We were spared when a German soldier of higher rank put a stop to the executions.[309]

Spared the fate of so many other POWs at the hands of the SS, Carvell now had to survive being a prisoner. The Germans quickly moved the POWs away from the front lines to make it difficult for the prisoners to get back their units. The prisoners began their journey to the POW camp Rennes just south of Normandy, the camp was also known as Stalag 133. The city contained a POW transit camp and POW hospital, which the Germans had been using since 1940. Rennes was just one of the many camps where members of Carvell's regiment were sent. Rifleman Edward Johnston of B Company RWR marched to Caen to be interrogated before marching to the Rheims camp.[310] He would face similar trials on the march that Carvell had on his way to Rennes.

CHAPTER SEVENTEEN

ELEVEN MONTHS AS A POW: CARVELL'S STORY

It took approximately eight days for Carvell's group to get to Rennes, France. During this first week of the march, Carvell noticed that there were few extra clothes and even less time to wash any that they had on them. He threw away his only pair of undershorts, leaving him with no undergarments or socks for this journey. He recalled, for the maltreatment form he filled out for the army, that for the first five days of the march he did not receive any food. The food that eventually did arrive was of terrible quality. It was soup made of old purple cabbage and water, and that was all that Carvell ate for three days. Then it changed to turnip soup.[311]

For the rest of his life, my great-great uncle George Carvell refused to eat turnips. This was one of the things that the family did know about his war experience. Perhaps he just had enough turnips to last him a lifetime. Or it could have been that the taste or smell evoked too many bad memories for him.

The prisoners were also given one loaf of black bread for the march. The Germans, on the other hand, had meat and bread for their meals. The Germans also had vehicles and bicycles for the journey, while Carvell and the others had to walk. Veness, Fairweather, and Learment marched to the same camp with a different group;[312] their route included going through Falaise, Vire, Flers, Ger, Mortain, and finally Rennes. Similar to Carvell, they went days without food and finally received soup and four-month-old bread.[313] The French underground sought to help the prisoners by giving them food as they marched through the villages.

Being on these marches was very dangerous for the Canadians. They had to watch out for their own planes firing at them in the belief that they were German soldiers on the march. Again against the Geneva Convention, the Germans did not allow the Canadians to wear their Red Cross armbands identifying them as allied POWs. Carvell said that they had to stand in the road while planes attacked his group. They were not allowed to take cover. Thirty-four men from Carvell's group were killed during the march.[314]

Not all German soldiers were as cruel as the ones in charge of Carvell's group. Those handling Veness and Fairweather's group warned them when a plane was coming back to attack, so they would be able to take cover. In Carvell's group, many men were wounded, and the Canadians were forced to look after their brothers in arms the best they could because the Germans would not care for them, even through the Geneva Convention requires that POWs receive medical care.[315]

Before reaching the camp, Carvell's group of prisoners stopped at a French Red Cross station in a village that was handing out soup and bread. The starved soldiers ate their portions quickly. Surviving the march was the main focus of most of the prisoners; however, escape was on their minds just as much. During this stop at the Red Cross, the Germans warned that if one man tried to escape, ten men would be shot in reprisal.[316] Again this would be a direct violation of the Geneva Convention to punish some soldiers for the actions of others. Soldiers who attempted escape could be brought before the courts for crimes or offences against persons or property committed in the course of such attempt. Fairweather had been told when he was in a lecture at a battle drill school in 1943 that it was his duty to escape if he were taken prisoner.[317] If they could not escape, they needed to help the war effort any way possible. This was most commonly done through acts of sabotage that the men performed while in captivity.

Carvell arrived at Rennes on 16 June 1944. Veness, Fairweather, and Learment's group had marched 135 miles in five days to get to the camp.[318] The German camp officials interrogated the Canadian officers upon their arrival and searched them again; however, the German Army had taken away all the Canadians' valuables when they were initially captured. After the interrogation and search, they were placed in their barracks. After his registration and placement, Carvell wrote a letter to his family, letting them know he was safe. His letter was brief, only containing three lines:

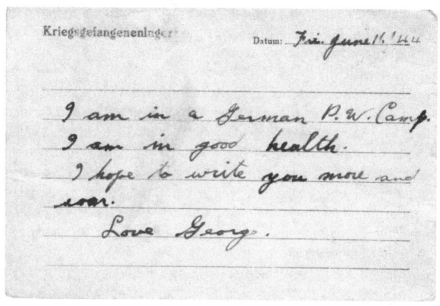

Figure 12: Carvell's first postcard home to his mother as a POW.
Author's personal collection.

Veness sent a letter home on the same day as Carvell: "Dear Mother, I am in a German P.W. Camp. I am in good health and will write more later. Love Jack."[319] Major L.D. Learment, of the North Novas, was also in the same camp and wrote his wife a letter, on 16 June 1944, very similar to Cavell and Veness: "I am in a German P.W. Camp. I am in good health. I will be writing you soon, Love Don."[320] These three letters, written by men not sitting together at the time of writing, are starkly similar. This could be because letters were often subject to censorship regarding what information they could contain, but the linguistic similarities here indicate that the prisoners were told what to write for this first letter.

The Canadian government sent a telegram to Carvell's mother on 25 June 1944, stating that Carvell had been officially reported Missing in Action on 8 June 1944. It read:

8147 Minister of National Defence deeply regrets to inform you that G 19455 Rifleman George William Carvell has been officially reported missing in action eighth June 1944 stop Further information becomes available it will be forwarded as soon as received. Director of Records.[321]

Being listed as Missing was often worse than being listed as a POW. Families would often assume that their family member was deceased when they were listed as Missing. They had to contend with the painful, faint hope that their loved one was indeed missing and not actually dead, but at the same time understand the reality that most missing in action had indeed died. The Saint John Telegraph Journal published notice Carvell was Missing in Action on 4 July 1944. He was one of many who were listed that day as a casualty. For as long as it took the letter that Carvell had written to reach his family, they were kept wondering as to where he was and if he was safe.[322] An official telegram telling his family that he was a POW was not sent until 20 November 1944.

Carvell spent several weeks in the Rennes camp, a large camp filled with Germans and a Gestapo Headquarters. There was a collection of worn-out army huts surrounded by three barbed wire fences. The barbed wire that surrounded the camp was approximately fifteen feet thick. There were guard towers at each corner, and guards patrolled the outside of the wire. The Germans did everything they could to discourage the prisoners from attempting escape.[323] There was a large building in the middle of the camp that had once been a drill hall.

The camp was divided into two parts, Caucasian prisoners on one side and what were then known as Negro prisoners on the other. Even though Carvell had a darker complexion than the norm, he was still placed with the Caucasian prisoners.[324] The Caucasian prisoners were treated better than the Negro prisoners. The Germans made the Negro prisoners turn over half their Red Cross supplies to the Caucasian prisoners, including cigarettes and candy. Their main meal was rice, while the

Caucasians often had stew.[325] The officers were placed in separate barracks from the other rank soldiers. The other rank prisoners stayed in larger huts with each soldier having their own bunk and blanket.[326]

It took some time for the soldiers to settle into some semblance of a routine in the camp. Veness and Fairweather recalled that they were allowed to take a shower once they arrived in the camp. Carvell recounted that he was only allowed to take three showers during his entire time in captivity.[327] Food was more available in the camps than on the march; however, the servings were still small compared to what the soldiers were used to. Breakfast rations consisted of two slices of bread with jam and something that resembled coffee. Lunch was often a stew of cabbage and rotten potatoes with a few beans added. There was occasionally a bit of meat in the stew, and the men gave it to a different person each time. Supper was just two slices of bread. The constant hunger made everything taste better than it would have under any other circumstance.[328]

Life in the prison camp could get monotonous, and the men often had to find things to keep them busy. The other rank soldiers had work to do around the camp, while the officers had more free time. Geneva Convention Article 27 states it states that prisoners could be used for work as long as it did not help the war effort. Officers could ask for work but would not be forced and NCOs would take supervisory work unless they requested otherwise. The soldiers would use anything they could find to make games. Veness and Fairweather made a checker board out of singles and the checkers from a broom.[329] Some of the French physicians working at the hospital would smuggle in playing cards and books for the prisoners. The men still played sports when they could. The lack of food often left them without the energy they'd had in Britain; however, sports gave them a break from the boredom they were experiencing. Boredom made many of the men contemplate escape. Some of the British paratroopers began digging a tunnel in their hut. When one of them was caught digging, he was placed under solitary confinement for two weeks.

The prisoners also tried to find out news of the war. The French citizens living around the camp did their best to provide information to the soldiers.[330] While new information was difficult to get, the prisoners often heard the frequent air raids occurring in proximity of the camp. As they could hear the raids and they had confidence of the initial Normandy landings, many believed that the Allies were going to win the war and that they would be liberated. There were, however, some worries that if the SS Divisions were pushed back to Rennes, that they would shoot all the prisoners before retreating further.[331]

Near the end of June, rumours surfaced that the prisoners would be moved to another camp. These proved to be true, and the camp inhabitants, including Carvell, Veness, and Fairweather were moved to a compound in Germany. The prisoners travelled by freight train, consisting of about fifteen French box cars with "40 Hommes, 8 Cheveaux" lettered on the sides.[332] The cars had two doors, one of which was padlocked, and two small windows on each side that were covered in wire. The German guards rode in passenger cars for the journey. The prisoners had to march a mile to get to the trains.

The officers rode in separate cars from the other ranks. Veness and Fairweather were in the same car, along with twenty-four officers and seven sergeants, leaving little room for any of them. Learment was in another car with last of the officers and sergeants. He managed to keep one of the maps that belonged to an American pilot, which he used to track their journey on the train. Carvell ended up in a different car with approximately thirty other men. There were other cars that had over forty people crammed into them. Carvell recalled his experience on the train, saying that there was "not enough room for all to sleep at once. Half would sit up while the others slept on the bare floors."[333] Veness and Fairweather described similar situations for sleeping in their car. Everyone found that it was best to sleep on their sides so each man had space to actually lie down.[334] The train did not leave the station until that night, as it had to travel at night and on a direct route. Travelling at night was safer because it was harder for planes to target them than in the daytime.

Apart from crowding there were numerous issues on the trains. Bathroom facilities consisted of a 45-gallon drums that were cut in half in each of the cars that were to be used for a toilet. Carvell described that they had no toilet privileges while on the train.[335] The constant stopping and starting of the train often led to the contents spilling on the floor or on the soldiers. When the train stopped at a station, volunteers needed to empty the drums. Food was another issue that was never fully addressed. Carvell described that there was never enough to eat. They would go two to three days without food or water. When food did come, the rations were small and meant to last numerous days. They were given half a loaf of black bread and a bit of sausage when they first entered the train.

Veness recalled how eating became a ritual for the men.[336] Each tried to ration the food to let them have three meals a day for the three days. Gobbling up the food as soon as they received it showed the animalistic nature of the situation, a sign that they were letting go if their self-control and their humanity. Veness and Fairweather both tried to restrain themselves from doing this. The soldiers received more food from Red Cross nurses who were at the stations when they stopped. On one occasion, they were able to get off the train and go to a wash station after the Red Crosses nurses complained to the German officials about the condition of the men.[337] On the journey, they had to stop the train numerous times because of the air raids and because the engines were needed elsewhere. On one occasion, the train stopped at Les Ville auz Dames for ten days. The men were not allowed out of the cars while they were stopped. The French Red Cross supplemented their food supplies with soup every day while they waited to move.[338]

Conditions deteriorated as they continued their journey. Many men began trying to find ways that they could escape off the train and get to the French underground. Escaping posed many risks and was not easy to achieve, especially on the train. Corporal Wesley Lebarr was able to escape from the train by prying some of the boards off the side of the car with a bar that he'd received from a farmer.[339] Veness and Fairweather decided to escape from their car. Like Lebarr, they had pried some of the boards from the car to make a hole they could get out of. A small group made their escape with Veness and Fairweather. All the men managed to get to the French underground. Learment was able to also escape from the train by making a bigger hole in the car that had been damaged and not fixed well. Unlike the others, Carvell did not escape from the train. He decided to stay where he was at instead of taking the chance of escaping and being killed for doing so. He spent twenty-seven days on the train before arriving at Stalag 12 D on 26 July.

Stalag 12 D was located in Waldbreitbach, Germany, near Neuwied. This was the second camp of four in which Carvell would be placed. He wrote another letter home while at this camp. This letter was longer than his first one. Again, he stated that he was doing well and hoped the family was the same. The only thing that he complained about was there was not enough smokes and they were difficult to obtain, saying "Dear Mother, just a line to let you know I am quite well and hope you are the same. About the only thing that is hard is smokes."[340] The Germans moved Carvell to another camp after he spent two months at Stalag 12 D. He stayed in this third camp only a few days before they moved him moved to Falkenau 13 B camp at the end of September. This would be Carvell's home until April 1945.

While marching to these different camps, Carvell had to go through German towns. He recalled their interactions with the children in the towns, saying "children along the way would throw anything at us that they could get their hands on. They'd even spit on us. But I don't blame the children, they were only doing what they had been taught."[341] The marches were difficult enough without the abuse they took while traveling through towns. Finally staying in one camp for longer than a few weeks took away some of the danger and abuse to which Carvell and the other men were subjected.

Falkenau 13 B camp was located in the Sokolov District of what is now the Czech Republic. It was a sub-camp of the Flossenburg Concentration Camp, which was located in Germany. My great-great Uncle George did not know at the time that the camp that he would spend six months in was, actually, a concentration camp where Jewish people were being exterminated.

He never spoke of this camp or any of the camps. The only information he provided about the camps was on his War Claims Commission form. It was very difficult to find out any information about the Falkenau camp. There is very little written on the facility, and what is written is not easy to locate. The information that I was able to find was from the memoirs of an American soldier who liberated this camp in May 1944. I was shocked to discover that the camp Uncle George spent the most time in (Falkenau) was connected to a concentration camp. It was even more of a shock to see some sources state that Falkenau was a concentration camp and not just a sub-camp to one.

As I shared this news with the family, they, like I, were shocked to learn that Uncle George had been in a camp were Jewish people and POWs from Eastern Europe and Russia were being tortured and killed. He never made mention any of this information. It may be that he was trying to spare us from the worst of his suffering, allow us some of the innocence that he was denied so long ago. Even in the newspaper article that discussed his wartime experience in detail, Uncle George did not mention what took place in the camps, only what happened on the marches.

Falkenau was located a few thousand yards from the town. It was surrounded by barbed wire barriers and had two main watchtowers. The sign that was placed on the doors of the camp read "Konzentrationslager Falkenau."[342] Carvell did what was required of him while in the camp. He had daily work to complete, and if he did not meet his quota, he would not get his food rations. All he wanted was to get back home to his family. He continued to write letters home as often as he was allowed. Carvell wanted to be home for Christmas 1944, but he knew that was not going to occur that year. Again, his main complaint of the camps by early December 1944 was the lack of cigarettes and clothing:

Dear Mother, Just a line to let you know I am well and hope you are the same. I would have love to be home for xmas but I guess not this year. It is not to bad here considering the smokes are scarce and so is the clothing but otherwise its not bad. Love George.[343]

He continued to be positive even when things were bad. His next letter home was in January 1945. This letter was very similar to the previous one, except he wrote that they were finally receiving more cigarettes. He also makes mention of the weather for the first time in his letters.[344] The last letter that Carvell's mother received from him as a POW was in February 1945. This letter appears to be written by someone else as it is not written in George's hand. The language and words used in the letter are the same as the others, so Carvell might have dictated the letter, or was forced to write in blocked letters:

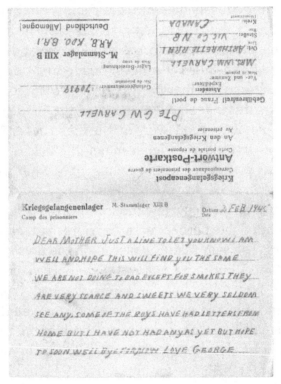

Figure 13: The last letter Carvell's mother received while Carvell was a POW, 1945. Author's personal collection.

All of the letters were very positive in nature, with only minor complaints. Either George was aware that the censors would be examining his communication home, or he simply did not want to upset his mother.

As the war was coming to an end in 1945, things began to change within all the prison, labour, and concentration camps. The Germans began evacuating the camps, and the prisoners began forced marches, which became known as the death marches because so many died on the journey. The Germans evacuated the camps because of the front lines of the war were moving and they needed to keep their prisoners from getting back to their militaries. Many camps in Germany were evacuated before the camps in Czechoslovakia; this explains why Carvell stayed in his camp until the spring. The Red Cross parcels that had kept most of the men alive during the war stopped arriving at the camps, and anything extra that the prisoners had received was no longer available. Both Dieppe and Normandy POWs were forced on these marches. Some of the camps began the evacuations mid-January, while others were not evacuated until April, including Carvell's camp.

The Dieppe prisoners in Stalag VIIIB were given little notice of the camp's evacuations. Many of the men went through what little possessions that they had and chose what they would take with them.[345] The men were given next to nothing for information about where they were going or how long they would be marching. With the below zero temperatures and snow up to four feet high, the POWs knew they needed to bring anything that would keep them warm. The Germans passed out what was left of the Red Cross parcels as the men were leaving the camps. These parcels were frozen from sitting outside; however, they took whatever food they could grab. Poolton left on the second day of evacuation. He recalled seeing men who had left the previous day lying dead and frozen on the side of the road.[346]

The conditions and treatment on the marches deteriorated rapidly. The men were forced to walk twenty to thirty kilometres a day, only stopping at night for sleep. Generally, they slept outside in the open although there were times when they could sleep in a barn or building if it was available. Many men died from exposure on the march, and parts of their bodies froze during the night if the men did not keep moving. The Germans would not let them start fires to keep warm or to dry their clothes. Poolton describes how he would place his wet socks on his stomach at night to dry using his body heat.[347] The prisoners continued to use whatever means were necessary to survive. The Red Cross parcels that the men received before leaving the camp was the only food they had until they reached another POW camp. When the march continued, they received bread rations every four or five days. The rations were insufficient for anyone to survive on, let alone men who were marching twenty to thirty kilometres a day in bitter winter weather. The men supplemented their rations with anything they could find, including food from the villagers, finding supplies the side of the road, and digging vegetables out of fields when the weather warmed. Everyone highly disapproved of stealing food from other soldiers, and few men resorted to this level.[348] While many of the Dieppe POWs were trying to survive the marches, Carvell was still at his camp in Czechoslovakia trying to survive there. Supplies for both the Germans and POWs were running thin because of war. Carvell continued doing what was required of him so he could get back to his family. He did not know that in a few short months he would leave the security of the camp and be on one of the marches.

The Germans were also evacuating the concentration camps as the front lines of the war advanced. Poolton recalled passing a group of Jewish people also on a death march. They were wearing striped prison uniforms, and many did not have any shoes for their feet. Seeing this, Poolton stated "one feels humble knowing that if it wasn't for the uniform we were wearing, we might have been in the same state."[349] Poolton realized that there was respect in wearing the uniform, and the Germans could have easily treated the Canadians as they did the Jewish people. The Jewish marches were a march of attrition. The Germans hoped to kill as many as they could. Many Jewish people who were sick or weak were shot before the march began. [350] Those who could not keep up were killed on the side of the road and just left there. The Germans gave no food on the march and took their blankets from them.[351] When the Jewish prisoners were able to get food, they needed to eat it immediately otherwise they risked being killed over their food. Many died from exposure and exhaustion, as did the POWs.

The SS continued to view the Jewish people not as human beings and believed that they should be made to suffer. In one instance, the Hitler Youth chased 5000-6000 Jews into a barn and set it on fire.[352] These acts of depravity were only some examples of what the Jewish people experienced before their liberation. Some of the Jewish people were liberated in April 1945; others had to wait until May before liberation finally occurred. The hope to be reunited with their loved ones is what kept many of the Jewish people from surrendering.

Memories of loved ones were also what kept most of the Canadians going on these marches. Carvell was lucky that he was not forced out of the camps at the beginning of 1945 like many others. For Poolton and the other men who had been marching since January, liberation could not come soon enough. Those who were not evacuated from the camps until spring endured less hardships, but still experienced adversity. The Germans had been holding out in Czechoslovakia. The armies had been surrendering in Denmark, Holland, and throughout the North. Carvell left Falkenau on 2 April 1945. Only a portion of the camp was evacuated and sent on a forced march. For this march, Carvell and his group walked for four or five days straight, only stopping for food and sleep. The men had no shelter from the elements or protection from the war, "We slept right in the open during those marches; all we had was our own 'smarts,' the only times we had any shelter for sleeping was after we had worked all day."[353] When they had shelter for sleeping, it was nothing more than big old brick buildings with dirt floors and barred-up windows.

Conditions were similar to the march that Carvell did when he was first captured. Many Canadians were shot by their own planes because they were mistaken as Germans. During the march, the men continued to do the work that the Germans required of them. Carvell described doing surface coal mining.

They would usually work for about a week before continuing marching.[354] The prisoners were given food rations if they met their daily work quota. Carvell, who was young and strong and still in relatively decent physical condition, would often help the others in the group make their quotas so no one would go without their rations. While the rations hardly filled the men's bellies, they were better than nothing.

The Germans continued to tell the prisoners that they were winning the war and that their imprisonment would be indefinite, and they would spend the rest of their lives under German authority. However, the Allied air raids were constant and difficult to not notice, so the prisoners knew that their captors were lying and that rescue would eventually arrive; the task was to survive until that happened

They continued marching between twenty and thirty kilometres a day. The prisoners were always on foot while the Germans had bicycles and trucks for transportation. There was little to no medical attention on the march. Carvell got painful blisters all over his feet that required aid, but he received none.[355] He had to make do with what he had or could find on the march to help ease some of the pain. Even with the lack of food and medical aid, Carvell continued to push through, knowing that his liberation would occur soon. Carvell recalled vividly his liberation when interviewed for the newspaper in 1994:

We were in Czechoslovakia when we were rescued. The Germans had kept telling us they were winning the war, but we knew different by the planes flying overhead and by the way the Germans kept us moving. The night before our rescue, we had slept in a big old barn. When we woke up in the morning, the Americans were just there. [356]

George Carvell and his comrades in arms were liberated by the First Infantry Division (the Big Red One) of the Third United States Army on 6 May, 1945. Just a few days after he was liberated, the Americans liberated Falkenau.[357] Many Germans were fleeing the Russians and wanted to surrender to the Americans rather than the Russians. The Germans knew that the Russians knew how the

Germans treated their Russian prisoners in the prisoner camps and did not want the same to happen to them. They also had more respect for the Americans than the Russians.

When the Americans arrived at Falkenau, they saw the horrors that the Canadians POWs had endured during their time there. Samuel Fuller, of the First Infantry Division, shot a twenty-two-minute film on the aftermath of the liberation of this camp. The Canadians were not the only men at the camp. Fuller recalled that the prisoners represented up to twelve different countries including Jews, Poles, Russians, Gypsies, and Americans.[358] He also stated that it was difficult to identify the American corpses without their dog tags. The Americans found many people within the camp extremely malnourished and in terrible condition. The barracks contained men and women with hollow eyes, unable to move their emaciated bodies. They had been tortured, beaten, and experimented upon.

In another building, the Americans found corpses thrown on top of one another, and there were some who were not dead yet but crying out for help. There were also many camp victims who had not been buried, but just thrown aside on top of one another. Fuller described the stench of rotting bodies that welled up in his face and made him want to stop breathing.[359] Throughout the camp, there were heaps of items taken from the camp victims including teeth, toothbrushes, eyeglasses, shaving brushes, and artificial limbs.[360]

The horrors of the camp culminated when they reached the crematorium. The crematorium contained four ovens and still contained the evidence of victims burning in them when the camp was liberated. Fuller's captain instructed him to capture these sights on film as well as the burial of the victims by the townspeople.[361] With the town of Falkenau so close to the camp, it was difficult to understand how the citizens did not know what was taking place in the camp. Most denied knowing that anything was taking place in the camp and that they were not Hitler supporters. Fuller's captain did not believe that they had known nothing. The Americans wanted to capture the evidence of the Nazi brutality to make sure that it could not be denied by the Nazis later.[362] Fuller's account states that the images of this camp haunted him for the rest of his life. If Fuller was haunted by what he saw after liberating the camp, one could only surmise the images that were left with Carvell and the others who had lived there for months. These horrors that Carvell witnessed would stay with him for the rest of his life, too.

The Americans came in trucks, tanks, and on foot to liberate the POWs. Carvell recalled that they treated them like family, gave them food and medical attention, and wanted to get the men back to Britain. They ensured that they men would not have to walk to get their freedom. Carvell got a plane ride back to Britain and was admitted into the hospital in Bramshot on 14 May 1945. His family received a telegraph on 17 May 1945, letting them know that he was safe in Britain:

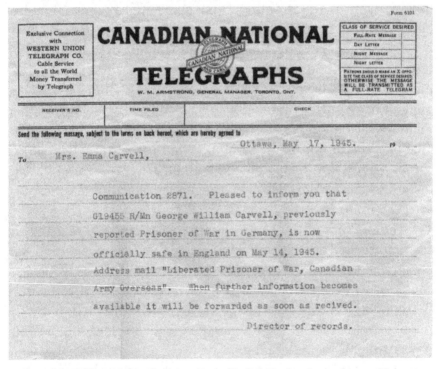

Figure 14: Telegraph informing Carvell's family that he had been liberate and was safe in Britain, 1945. Author's personal collection.

Carvell had lost sixty pounds during his time as a POW. The doctors noted that his ankles, legs, and face were swollen, likely from the march. The doctor also noted that Carvell displayed a moderate degree of malnutrition.[363] While Carvell was recuperating, he told the doctors that he contracted jaundice at the camps and did not receive any medical aid.[364] He had been forced to work even while sick, which was against his rights as per the Geneva Convention. But he'd done it, and he had survived.

Over a month and a half of good medical care, sanitary conditions, and nutritious meals, Carvell regained his health and even some of the weight he had lost. Finally, after over three years in Europe, George Carvell was going home.

CHAPTER EIGHTEEN

THE CANADIANS GO HOME

The German surrender on 7 May 1945 signalled the end of combat for thousands of Canadians overseas. The war in Europe was finally over. Wild celebrations broke out in the streets of Canada and around the world, but not everyone was celebrating the end of the war.

The cost would still need to be paid, particularly by those who had endured being in combat. Exhausted soldiers did not celebrate; rather, their thoughts were on the countless comrades who were taken from them and the question of what they were going to do with the rest of their lives. There were also 44,000 Canadian families who had lost loved ones during the years of combat who did not know how to mark the end of the nightmare.[365] Those families did not know if they should celebrate that no more families would have to read that dreaded telegram stating that their loved one had been killed in action or grieve for the loss they had felt since they had received their own notice.

While the celebrations of the war's end raged on, the Canadian government had the monumental task of demobilizing the quarter of a million men and getting them back home. Some of these men had spent six years of their lives overseas and were anxiously waiting to set foot on Canadian soil again. The government put in a system based on points as to who would be sent home first. This system took into account the length of service and prioritized men, attempting to ensure that there was a "first in, first out" policy.[366] Many of the overseas units began losing their most experienced rank and file with this policy. The government also asked for volunteers to serve in the Canadian Division that would be a part of the invasion of the Japanese home islands. These volunteers were given thirty days' leave to go back to Canada before heading to the Pacific theatre. While most soldiers wanted to go home, they quickly realized that there would be a long wait for that ship.

The soldiers were not the only ones who were looking forward to getting to Canada. Thousands of soldiers had married during their time in Britain and looked to Canada to start their new lives. From August 1941 to January 1947, 41,251 wives and 19,737 children made the trip across the Atlantic to start their new lives in Canada.[367]

Once the soldiers finally got that ship back home, they were faced with the homecomings. With the points system sending men home, individual service personnel were welcomed home; however, the regiments, squadrons, or ships for the most part could not be celebrated as a whole.[368] Most soldiers arrived in Canada, docked in Halifax, and then traveled by rail to cities and towns across the country. Homecoming produced mixed feelings for those arriving. Some felt regret for not keeping in contact with their families as much as they should have while overseas. Others were given a hero's welcome when they did not believe they deserved such treatment.[369]

None of them came back to a home and a family that had been exactly as it was when they had left. Homecoming veterans would see new lines on their mothers' faces, less hair on their fathers' heads, children who were much bigger than when they'd left. If those children had been very young, they may not have remembered their daddies at all. Some men met their children for the first time, having left while their wives were still expecting. Those children might have been a few years old before the men had held them for the first time, knowing that they never saw the first step or heard the first word, because their children lived their first few years without them. The men would go back to wives who had developed new independence and resilience in the war years they'd had to manage the household alone. In spite of the changes in circumstances, these reunions were usually joyful and loving.

It was, overall, bittersweet for the veterans. They were happy and thankful that they had survived captivity but they had to adjust to a very different life upon returning to Canada. The overseas personnel were greeted as conquering heroes, but what was it like coming home as a defeated warrior? Canadians had a difficult time understanding a fighting soldier's experience; the POW experience was completely foreign to them. A post war study revealed that 48% of Dieppe prisoners had psychological problems adjusting to life back home, and most prisoners from the other battles were similarly traumatized.[370]

Soldiers arriving home remained members of the armed services until their discharges came through. They were permitted thirty days' leave while their paperwork was completed. The government gave out booklets to the returning men and women that informed them what to expect when they arrive home and of what resources were available to them during this time. During this time, the troops underwent final medical and dental examinations and received opportunities for counselling. Very few decided to talk to the psychologists for fear it would delay their return to civilian life.[371] In the forties, medical professionals and society in general did not have the understanding we do now about post-traumatic stress or the importance of psychological support for combat veterans. Rather, the focus was more often to simply put it behind you and start building your life again. The government provided numerous programs for veterans to start their new lives including re-training programs, education funding, and business funding. Many men went back to the jobs that they'd had before the war, while others decided to take the government funding and start their lives in a new direction.

Each soldier had a different experience during the war, and each had a different homecoming. The transition back to civilian life was easy for some, slipping seamlessly back into their families and jobs, while others struggled daily with what they had witnessed and endured overseas.

The Canada to which they came home was a very different Canada from which they had left. Women had new roles, new confidence, and new independence. Numerous veterans had come back physically or mentally injured, and they would no longer be able to function independently. Most families were happy to have their loved ones back regardless of their injuries and provide loving care. There were many families who had lost loved ones, and they would have given anything to have them back even if they were not the same. All of these people, the families, the veterans (injured or not), were part of Canadian society and they had to figure our how to live together and help one another begin their lives once again.

Chapter Nineteen

The Timber Man's Homecoming

George Carvell sailed home on the SS Louis Pasteur, arriving in Halifax on 1 July 1945, after seven days at sea. He arrived in Plaster Rock just two days later. His family was there to finally be reunited with him. His whole family made sure to be in attendance, including his little 5-year-old niece, Arlene, to welcome him home..

It was a bittersweet moment for the family. They had lost over three years with him and at times, did not know if they would ever see him again and prepared themselves for the possibility that they would never see him again. Now that he was finally home, they were aware that his experiences he had overseas made him a different man. Gone was the young, innocent child; in his stead, was a man who saw and experienced more atrocities than they could ever understand. They would have to get to know their loved one all over again, and perhaps never fully understand why he was different. But for Uncle George, this was the moment when he would finally be able to begin his life; start a career, get married, and have his own family. He also quickly saw that life had not stopped while he had been overseas. His siblings had grown and moved on with their lives. Carvell's eldest sister, Thelma, was getting married in a few months, and his second youngest sister, Christina, planned to marry early the following year.

Carvell himself wasted no time getting his own life going. He applied for retraining in motor mechanics through the Department of Veterans Affairs. "He seems very enthusiastic about this type of work," his counsellor wrote on his DVA application, "and it is felt that he has sufficient education and ability to complete the course successfully."[372] With this new training and the training he'd undergone while in Britain, Carvell was able to get a job driving truck for a local company. He stayed with that company until 1951. Also during this time, he was self employed as a carpenter until he obtained a job as a millwright at Fraser's Mill in Plaster Rock in 1951He worked at the mill until his retirement in 1986.[373]

After all his years at the mill, Carvell developed the hobby of woodworking. He made many items for members of his family and community, including shelves, nightstands, and duck banks. Carvell continued with many of the hobbies that he had before the war, including hunting and four-wheeling. He was even a member of the local four-wheeling club.

Figure15: Duck bank and cabinet that George Carvell made.
Author's personal collection

Transitioning back to civilian life was not as simple for many other returning veterans, however. While many were trying to make this transition, they were also dealing with varying degrees of battle exhaustion, now known as Post-Traumatic Stress Disorder Though George Carvell's shift seemed smooth on the surface, he did realize that he was also dealing with battle exhaustion. Not every soldier who went into war suffered from crippling battle exhaustion. Copp and McAndrew argue that each soldier entering a battle carries within himself a varying degree of predisposition or vulnerability to combat stress, which may or may not lead to breakdown, depending on numerous factors, not excluding the fortunes of war.[374] Each soldier could sustain a certain amount of trauma (combat or captivity) before reaching their breaking point. Once the soldier reached that breaking point, they needed to have support in place to help them either get back into battle or be able to function in society. Carvell recognized that he suffered from this after the war and needed help to cope properly. He never turned to his family for support even though they supported him. He turned to his friends from the war, used his time in the woods to help, or at times coped in silence.

Battle exhaustion was not a new problem for the military. Authorities and medical personnel had witnessed it in the First World War, and they had tried to find ways to deal with it during the Second World War. In the First World War, the condition was known as shell shock, a nervous disorder that was difficult for military physicians to diagnose and to cure. Shell-shocked men did not exhibit consistent symptoms. The issues ranged from shaking hands, tremors, sleepless nights, delusions, and paralysis of limbs. It wasn't until halfway through that war that doctors regarded this as a psychological disorder and found new treatments. Doctors found that soldiers needed rest and recuperation to get back to the front lines. Due to the number of soldiers needed for battle, most soldiers did not get the rest the needed. To get soldiers back to the front lines more quickly, authorities used electric shock therapy.[375] Approximately 9000 Canadians were diagnosed with shell shock during the First World War. Researchers estimate that more than 15,000 actually had it, however, many were killed before being officially diagnosed.[376] After the war, many men developed nervous and mental disorders, and they needed professional help to manage their conditions.

When the Second World War broke out, the military knew it had to approach the issues of shell shock in a different way to reduce the rate of cases from that of the previous war. Historians Copp and McAndrew argue that each soldier had an individual breaking point regarding the amount of trauma they could sustain before needing treatment or support.[377] Men could only take the strain of harsh living, constant stress, poor food, lack of sleep, and carnage before they broke down. During the Italian campaign, 5020 casualties received the label of "neuropsychiatric," amounting to 16.9 percent of the total casualties.[378] Treatments were very similar during the Second World War as they were during the First. Rest and recuperation were the main treatments; however, military medical personnel also used electric shock therapy when they believed it to be necessary. Soldiers were often more easily able to get treatment while in combat than they were after the war. Support for veterans was especially important after the war. This support was often lacking because of the delayed responses of battle exhaustion from the war. The treatments and supports that are available for soldiers now were not available to Carvell and the veterans of the Second World War. Most often veterans went to the Legion to talk to their comrades who went through similar experiences to get some solace. The Department of Veterans Affairs did create a department to treat men who suffered from battle exhaustion; however, most men did not go there to seek treatment.

Historian Tim Cook points out that while war lingered on the minds of men, most veterans were not in turmoil and should not be depicted as victims just because they served.[379] Carvell easily fit into this category. He faced many challenges after coming home; however, he did not let that stop him from living his life to the fullest.

Uncle George saw his siblings settling down, getting married, and having children. He wanted all of these things too. He began courting Bernice Lovean after he came home from the war. They had known each other before the war; however, it was not until after uncle George came home that their relationship began.

On 3 July, 1946, one year to the day that he arrived back home from the war, he wed Bernice. Reverend Chapman officiate the ceremony at the Primitive Baptist Church in Plaster Rock. Uncle George and Bernice had their family and friends there to witness and celebrate their wedding. Finally, Uncle George was starting the life that he wondered during this imprisonment if he was going to have.

Uncle George and Bernice have one child, Sandra, who was born on 31 March, 1947. They watched her get married to Philip Crawford on 24 August 1968. They have three children.

Carvell's war experiences never left him. This is evident on 27 January 1948, when he reenlisted in the local militia. He had only formally been discharged on 29 August 1945. Just over two years later, he decided to sign up with the Carlton & York Regiment in the Canadian Army Reserve. He enlisted with the rank of private, but quickly received a promotion to corporal by May 1948.[380] Carvell trained with C Company based in the regions of Grand Falls and Plaster Rock area. He completed 30 days local HQ training in December 1948. The Historical Reports of the regiment provided descriptions of the yearly happenings of the companies,[381] including Remembrance Day ceremonies and numerous sports leagues. He had enjoyed playing sports before and during the war, and he continued playing softball and basketball through the militia leagues. Carvell stayed in the militia for twelve years. During that time, he completed a significant amount of training, rose to the rank of sergeant, and served as a training instructor near the end of his military career.[382]

Figure 16: Carvell (last in first group) marching with the militia, 1958. Author's personal collection.

Carvell used his military experiences to help promote re-membrance within his community. With an active role in the local Legion, he continued his participation in the yearly Remembrance Day ceremonies even after leaving the militia. In 1994, Carvell, with his wife at his side, returned to France for the 50th anniversary of the Normandy invasion. He was reunited with fellow veterans of the invasion and some of the men who had been prisoners with him. It was deeply emotional to go back to the beaches and to Beny-sur-Mer Canadian War cemetery. Carvell later commented, "It was hard walking through the rows of graves noting the ages of all the young soldiers buried there."[383] He went to visit the grave of his friend William Smith, with whom he had grown up. He also visited the memorial for the Royal Winnipeg Rifles located on the seafront of Courseulles-sur-Mer. The tour also took them to Britain, Belgium, Germany, and Holland.

Figure 17: Carvell at the Royal Winnipeg Rifle's memorial
in Courseulles-sur-Mer, France, 1994. Author's personal collection.

In 2007, Carvell began going to Donald Fraser Memorial school, the local elementary school in Plaster Rock, with Eldred Bucci, another veteran. Knowing that the Second World War would soon disappear from living memory, they spoke to the students about the importance of remembering the war and the veterans. They did their best to put a face and a reality to what those children only knew as stories in a textbook or television. The teacher, Susan Harrison, had taken part in the Juno Beach Centre Professional Development Tour for educators in 2007, and she believed in the importance of remembrance for the next generation.[384] Both Carvell and Bucci were regular visitors to the school and helped with any remembrance-related projects.

My great-great uncle, George Carvell, passed away on 30 November 2009, at the age of 86, and he was laid to rest beside his wife. His wife passed away in 1999. He was the last member of his generation of the family. The large number of people at who attended the viewings and funeral gave evidence to the impact that Carvell had on his community and showed that he would be greatly missed. Along with the family, many who travelled from all over the country, many members of the Legion, students from the elementary school, members from the Knights of Columbus, and others from the community paid their last respects. The family and community grieved the loss of a great man, but they celebrated the full life he had lived and the service he'd given to his family, his occupation, his community, his nation, and the world.

Figure 18: Carvell, 2009. Author's personal collection

CHAPTER 20

COMPLETING THE CIRCLE

I applied for the Canadian Battlefields Foundation's 2014 study tour after discussing the opportunity with a couple of my professors (Dr. Milner and Dr. Windsor). The Canadian Battlefields Foundation offers scholarships to twelve Canadian students to travel to Europe to visit the battlefields of the First and Second World War. The mandate of the foundation is to increase public education on the remembrance of Canada's role in war and military operations since the beginning of the 20th Century through its battlefields study tours, other educational activities, and commemorative events.[385] The tour that they offer to students slightly varies each year but looks at the battles of the First and Second World War. This tour would spend the majority of the tour focusing on the Normandy Campaign because it coincided with the 70th anniversary of the campaign.

With the focus on the tour being the Normandy Campaign, both of my professors believed that this would be an excellent way to add some real-life experiences to the writing of my thesis. When I received the call telling me that I'd been chosen for the trip, I was ecstatic. After years of wishing, I was finally going to Europe and I would be the first in the family to go on this very special journey. As the initial excitement eased into reflection, I began to ponder the incredible importance of this opportunity not only for my academic career but also for my family and for my own personal memory and desire to honour my great-great uncle.

In my application, one of the reasons I explained for wanting to go on the trip was the family connection I had.. I told them the story of my great-great uncle George's time in Europe during the forties as well as that he'd done the Veterans' tour in 1994 and was present at Juno Beach for the 50th Anniversary. I had pictures of him at the beach and at the Royal Winnipeg Rifles' memorial. I knew those were two of the places that I needed to visit on my travels. I would also be able to see his brick at the Juno Beach Centre that his daughter had purchased for him. I was looking forward to getting some pictures to send back to her, because she had never seen the brick before.

It was only after this initial excitement had subsided that I realized that twenty years later the tour I would be attending would be a larger one that uncle George had completed. The realization that it was twenty years between tours really hit me. It was though things were coming around full circle by me taking this trip, that I would be able to fully connect with this profound and extraordinary part of him that I'd been seeking out through my time working on my thesis. I hoped that he would have been proud of what I was doing.

Walking the battlefields that Uncle George fought on helped me to understand what he went through, as well as the story of the Canadians during the Normandy invasion. I spent fifteen days travelling around Belgium and France during the Canadian Battlefields Foundation Tour, touring the First World War and Second World War sites. Setting foot on the battlefields changed my perspective of the battles and gave me a much better understanding of what the men endured. Rather than considering the academics, I could see them walking, young and smooth-faced, wearing rumpled uniforms and carrying guns in hands. I understood more about the landings and how the odds they'd faced had been so daunting. Through the land was green, I could image the blood that much have soaked there, the mud and the debris. It smelled fresh and full of life, but I could image the stench of death and smoke and fear.

Even thought there were moments of profound grief as I took in the magnitude of what the soldiers endured and sacrificed, it was, for me, a joyful trip. When I arrived in France, I was beyond excited. I tried to take in as much as I could; however, I was anxiously waiting until we got to our Normandy Base. I knew when we got to the beach it would be emotional. Beny-sur-mer is the Canadian cemetery for those killed during the Normandy campaign. My mind kept going to the fact of how easily Uncle George could have been resting in that cemetery, the bones of a young man, instead of being in a cemetery back in New Brunswick, buried as an old man who had lived a long and fulfilling life. That cemetery is just one of the many cemeteries filled with men who were killed during the liberation of Europe. Seeing the over 2000 headstones of Canadians was surreal. Reading about the amount of men killed is completely different than actually seeing them in person. Two thousand is a large number, but it is difficult to really picture it until you walk into Beny-sur-mer. I was honoured to participate in the commemoration ceremony and lay a rose at the cross of sacrifice. While I was at the cemetery, I was able to visit one of my friend's relatives and also visit Uncle George's friend William Smith, who was killed during the Normandy Invasion. That young man's bones lay beneath the earth in France, an ocean away from where his friend would eventually lay, but Uncle George kept his memory alive, and I was grateful to be able to pay my respects.

The morning of 6 June, we headed to Juno Beach for the first of three ceremonies that day. The first ceremony was at the Queen's Own Rifles house (now called Canada's House). It was a touching ceremony. There was a large crowd gathered and there were current of the QOR as well as two French youth who pledged to carry the torch of remembrance for all the Canadians who gave their lives. After the ceremony, we had a little time to explore before moving on to the next part of the day. Most went to the beach to explore. It took me a few minutes before I could actually step out onto the beach.

I was about to set foot on hallowed ground.

Again, I imagined what my uncle and countless other men had to endure on that terrible, victorious morning over half a century ago. The deafening roar of machine gun fire, screams, surging bodies, the drive to *go! go! go!* even when every instinct must have screamed to *stay! stay! stay!* I could see the death that surrounded them, the blood, and the fear. It was utterly overwhelming. I was fortunate to have the support of my tour mates, who rushed to hug me when the tears started.

The main ceremony at the Juno Beach Centre was impressive. The program consisted of numerous speakers, songs, and collected memories of the sacrifices of so many men. The amount of people there to commemorate this anniversary was overwhelming. I had never seen so many people there to remember the sacrifices that so many of our men gave. It was a proud moment being there and being a Canadian. Both Prime Minister Harper and His Royal Highness Prince Charles gave wonderful speeches on the efforts of the Canadian Army and the sacrifices that were given. I also enjoyed hearing Major-General Richard Rohmer's D-Day story again. I'd been honoured to meet him the previous day at the Beny-sur-Mer ceremony. Hearing his story made me again think of my uncle George and what his thoughts would have been for this ceremony. It would have been interesting to compare his experiences at the 50th anniversary ceremony to mine at the 70th anniversary. One big difference was the number of veterans of the campaign. There would have been significantly more veterans at the 50th anniversary than the 70th. Even Major-General Rohmer stated that this anniversary would be the last decade ceremony that would have veterans present. I felt very lucky knowing that I could meet some of these veterans and hear their stories.

While 6 June was an emotional day because of being the first time at the beach, two days later turned into another one. The day turned into the Royal Winnipeg Rifles day. We started at the section of the beach that the Winnipegs landed. It was surreal standing on the beach that uncle George landed on. It was hard to focus on my tour-mate's presentation on the 7th Brigade because my mind kept going back to Uncle George and wondering what had been going through his mind when the door of the landing craft went down and he had to get up the beach. I brought some pictures of him with me so I could have pictures taken with him once again. It felt like, by doing that, he was back with me. When we got to the Juno Beach Centre, I was easily able to find his brick and get some pictures with it. I brought one of his pictures from when he was nineteen to place with the brick.

After a tour of the centre, we headed to the Royal Winnipeg Rifles memorial. I had pictures of uncle George at that memorial so that was one place that I needed to visit on the trip. I also got an arrangement of flowers to lay at the memorial. The only thoughts on my mind were my uncle and how twenty years ago he was at that place. It was an honour to lay the flowers there in his memory. Overwhelmed with emotion, I could not stop the tears. Again, I was fortunate to have such wonderful support from everyone I was with. We got some wonderful pictures while there and it felt great that I was able to be there. We got a few group pictures at the memorial before heading inland to discuss the D-Day + 2 battles.

When we arrived at Putot-en-Bessin, I did my last presentation on the efforts of the Royal Winnipeg Rifles during this battle. When we were picking out the presentation topics, Dr. Milner told me that I had to do one on the RWR at Putot since I had the connection there. It was amazing to be on the land that Uncle George was captured on. It has been difficult to describe what it was like being there. I found that with all the battlefields. It was hard to describe the effect of knowing that so many people lost their lives on the grounds. It was difficult to comprehend being there knowing that this ground was the beginning of the eleven months of Uncle George being a POW.

This tour really did complete the circle for me and my family. I was able to honour the memory of my uncle and show my family the area that played such an important role in his life. This tour will also be reflected in my thesis. It was not until I was able to actually see these sites that I was able to truly understand what the men went through and some of what my uncle experienced so many decades ago.

Figure 19: Placing flowers at the memorial for Uncle George, 2014.
Author's personal collection

Figure 20: My picture at the memorial, 2014.
Author's personal collection

One of the most important things I learned from this journey was the strength that Uncle George possessed to be able to endure surviving the Normandy invasion, living as a POW for eleven months, and coming home and starting a life that was so good and full of meaning. He demonstrated that soldiers could come back from the war not as victims but survivors, and they could maintain complete, meaningful lives that would nurture future generations.

ADDENDUM

RESEARCH ANALYSIS AND RECOMMENDATIONS FOR FUTURE READING

This book is adapted from the scholarly thesis I wrote for my Master's degree in History. As an academic work, it required significant analysis that goes beyond what may be of interest to the general public.

For those readers who are interested in a more comprehensive analysis of the research material, I've included some expanded discussion of my main sources and a list of recommended further reading. This following section appears much as the literature review found in my thesis.

As a writer and a scholar, I am fortunate to be able to learn from and borrow from the work of those who have examined this subject before me. The body of literature on the Normandy campaign is vast, including numerous documents about training for the operation and the invasion. We will examine this first. Second, we will look at what has already been written about POWs so that we might give Carvell's story that context. However, the body of Canadian literature on the prisoner of war experience is modest. The story of prisoners of war in Hong Kong and Dieppe are the most well-known. There exists little literature about the prisoners of war that were captured in Normandy. Most of what is written covers the murders of Canadian prisoners of war by the 12th SS Panzer Division (Hitler Youth).

Training the Canadian Army for this campaign took place over a four-year period while troops were stationed in Britain. The training that the Canadians received in Britain in the early years of the Second World War has been subjected to scrutiny. Historians have put some of the blame of Canada's apparent poor showing during the Normandy campaign on the inadequate quality of training that they received.[386] Carvell was in the 1st Canadian Reinforcement Unit for a year before moving to the 7th Infantry Reinforcement Unit. Canadian war literature often glosses over the Reinforcement Units. A scholar might ask many questions when examining the reinforcement units and the training they received overseas. What training did the units receive? What did the reinforcement units do when the regular regiments were involved in the large scale exercises? Did the regular regimental officers drop in to the reinforcement units to direct them in the newest training so these units would be in sync with all the others?

Colonel C.P. Stacey's *Six Years of War - The Army in Canada, Britain, and the Pacific* (1955) spends a significant amount of time describing the training the army received in Canada before leaving for Britain and while in Britain before going into action. His main focus is on the regular regiments, while glossing over the training the reinforcement units provided. The reinforcement units focused on training the individual as a soldier while the regular units trained them as a team. This individual training was essential for the units to function properly as a team. Stacey describes how training the reinforcement units was a different problem and required a special organization.[387] Most of the men coming into Britain with the reinforcement units were 'raw or nearly raw recruits.'[388] A regular course of training became required for all Canadian Holding Units. Stacey goes into detail of how the organization of the Reinforcement Units changed during its time in Britain, more than the actual training that they received.

While Stacey does gloss over the training of the reinforce-ment units, he describes the training of the regular units in detail. His main argument with the quality of the training the regiments received is that while he believes that the Canadians did well in Normandy, they would have done better had they not been fighting their first battle and learning as they fought.[389] Stacey examines the evolution of the training for the Canadians, moving from individual and collective training to battle drill to large-scale training exercises. It was during the large scale training exercises that the faults of the units came to light.

Training for the Normandy campaign changed from what the Canadians had been doing previously. Starting in 1943, the 3rd Canadian Infantry Division, of which the RWR was a part, began preparation for an assault on a heavily guarded beach. The first phase would be the preliminary training which involved the study of principles of combined operations and practice in embarkation and disembarkation, scaling obstacles, clearing minefields, etc. The second phase was basic training on the mechanics of assault landings. The third phase was increased realism with the assault training and the final phase was collective divisional assault training.[390] He also contends that a large proportion of regimental officers had a casual and haphazard attitude towards training, rather than an urgent and scientific one.[391]

Stacey says little about the reinforcement units. John A. English's *The Canadian Army and the Normandy Campaign: A Study of Failure of High Command* (1991) completely ignores them. English argues that it was high command's shortcomings that seriously impaired the Canadian fighting performance. The Canadian field force was compromised by a military leadership that had for too long concentrated on bureaucratic, political, stratego-diplomatic, and technical pursuits to the neglect of its operational and tactical quintessence.[392] English focuses in particular on the training that the officers and commanders received and the adaption of the battle drill training. The battle drill was a direct attempt to emulate the actions of German soldiers on the battlefield.[393] The author also focuses on battle inoculation and how the officers used this to impress the troops with exhibitions of their own toughness or frighten candidates beyond repair. He maintains that more time should have been spent on identifying enemy weapons by sight and sound than frightening the citizen army through battle inoculation. This adds to English's premise that the training of the officers was lacking and one of the main causes of his belief that the Canadians failed at Normandy.

The Canadian Army and the Normandy Campaign examines the individual and collective training that was given to the soldiers during the months before the Normandy invasion. The main priority during this training period was on the individual. This training was bringing the soldiers back to the basics. English states this was the last opportunity the commanders had to make the men fit to fight.[394] Even with this intense training period prior to the assault, battalions were still having problems.

English's text seeks to displace the myth that Canadian soldiers over-trained during the four years in Britain. He supports Stacey's conclusion that the large scale training exercises showed that the Canadians were not ready for a large attack.[395] He also criticizes General A.G.L. McNaughton's handling of the first Canadian Army and maintains that a lack or professional knowledge could have been rectified through study. English argues that the relatively lackluster showing of Canadian arms in Normandy must be laid at the feet of division commanders.[396] He contends that the Canadian infantry did not generally appear to have been as well trained as the Germans in fighting and skill.[397] He argues that it was the higher command which led to 'failures' in Normandy. These 'failures' were evident in the summer of 1944 when the Canadians failed to push forward as they should have. Some historians believed the Canadians missed many opportunities to close the Falaise Gap and achieve the objectives of Overlord.

Both Stacey and English provide accounts of what the Canadian army training in Britain entailed at the command level. Captain Harold MacDonald is able to bring the individual soldier perspective to this discussion. MacDonald wrote numerous letters to his wife while he was overseas during the war. These letters were published in the journal *Canadian Military History* in two separate articles (2006). These articles cover the two years that he spent in Britain training with the North Shore (NB) Regiment before entering the war during the Normandy campaign. As a rule, units arrived in Britain fully formed, often comprised of militia who had served together for years already. The RWR, for example, mobilized in May 1940 and arrived in Britain as a fully formed and unarmed infantry battalion on 12 September 1940. What they needed the most was training. The letters describe life for a Canadian soldier in Britain, from the leaves to London, the letter/parcels from home, to the training courses that he was on. The letters make clear the thoughts and feelings of MacDonald about his training and large scale exercises. They also show the effects of injuries had on soldiers while they recovered. While MacDonald's experience in Britain was different than Carvell's because MacDonald received officer training, there are links between the two men and what they experienced.

MacDonald's individual perspective is different than the operational and tactical perspective described by historians Stacey and English. While the larger perspective is important to understand the general themes, the individual experiences of the soldiers also tell a significant story. MacDonald's account provides insight into the larger picture by describing his battle inoculation[398] and participation in the large-scale exercises[399] that both Stacey and English describe.

There exists extensive literature on the Normandy campaign itself. Col. C.P. Stacey's third volume of the official history, *The Victory Campaign: The Operation in North-West Europe, 1944-1945,* (1960) examines the preparation for the Normandy invasion, the campaign, and the battles that led to the German surrender. The text details the information on the 7 Canadian Infantry Brigade's progress during the initial invasion in a few pages. When summarizing the day's events, Stacey comments that the D-Day achievement was magnificent; however, he quickly raises questions as to why more was not achieved that day.[400]

The advance on the final D-Day objectives on 7 and 8 June was significant for the Royal Winnipeg Rifles (RWR or Winnipegs), of the 7 Canadian Infantry Brigade. The Winnipegs took their final D-Day objective at noon on 7 June and dug in at Putot-en-Bessin. Stacey covers the subsequent counterattack by the Germans in a page, describing how quickly the Germans took back the area.[401] The Canadian Scottish Regiment helped the Winnipegs regain the town later in the day. Stacey praises the Canadian Scottish on their magnificent showing, exemplified in their ability to retake the town. He comments on the high causality toll this battle and counterattack had on the Winnipegs and Canadian Scottish, with only a brief mention of the Canadians who were murdered by the 12th SS Panzer Division.[402] Marc Milner critiques Stacey's attitudes toward these beachhead battles in his book *Stopping the Panzers: The Untold Story of D-Day*. He contends that Stacey and his staff were absorbed in the "failure to move forward" paradigm and they never knew the ultimate purpose of the Canadian assault.[403] Many of the documents that described the ultimate objectives of these battles were released years after Stacey wrote his official history. Stacey and his staff were also not very interested in the early defensive battles, which can be seen in how little they actually wrote in the official history on these battles even though they were significant to the achievement of the invasion. His descriptions of these battles echo the German criticism of the Allied infantrymen as being too hesitant and careful. Instead of praising the accomplishments, he simply lauds the men and their commitments.[404]

Stacey is highly critical of the Allies' showing at Normandy. He states that the Allied armies enjoyed the cooperation of very powerful naval forces and tremendous air forces that were constantly brought into play against the enemy troops on the ground.[405] The lack of battle experience undoubtedly had its effect on Canadian formations. Training, he insists, was a major issue. The Germans appeared to get more out of the training than the Canadians, as they showed themselves to be excellent practitioners of their trade.[406] Stacey praises Canadian generalship in Normandy and states that the Germans had been decisively outgeneralled. While he has great praise for the generals, the same cannot be said for the regimental officers.[407] He claims that the officers were not fully competent for their appointments, and their inadequacy appeared in action and sometimes had series consequences.[408] The critique of the Canadian failure to exploit their initial success and achieve their final objectives continues with the inability to capture Falaise quick enough in August, the inexperienced troops compared to the Germans, and the troubles the 2nd Canadian Infantry Division had.

Until recently, Stacey and English's analyses of the Canadians at Normandy has been the dominant paradigm for understanding the Canadian role in the campaign. Terry Copp changed the Normandy paradigm when he published his ground-breaking work *Fields of Fire: The Canadians in Normandy* (2003). Copp disagrees with Stacey's assessment that the Canadians had a lackluster showing and the Germans were a superior fighting force. He argues that the achievement of the Allied and Canadian armies in Normandy has been greatly underrated while the effectiveness of the German army has been greatly exaggerated.[409] He also argues that the air and naval power was far from the decisive factor in the Normandy invasion. Air power helped to weaken the enemy, but it was not decisive.[410] Stacey contends that the regimental officers in the army were not fully competent in their appointment. Copp questions this assertion and believes that the overwhelming majority of commanding officers were fully competent for their posts.

Copp provides detailed descriptions of the Normandy invasion and subsequent battles. He used message logs, war diaries, historical officer interviews conducted within days of the battle, written orders issued in the field, operational research reports, air photos and maps, and an intimate knowledge of the ground to paint the picture of what happened that day.[411] During the advance inland, the British and Canadians fought the way they had been trained, moving forward to their designated objectives in controlled bounds and digging in at the first sign of a counterattack.[412] This is a different stance than that of Stacey, who maintains that the Canadians failed due to their inability to capture their first day objectives. The Winnipegs, for example, fought with determination and success on D-Day but were overrun and virtually destroyed on D+2. This regiment fought bravely; however, their efforts are often overshadowed by the tragedy of 8 June—the day George Carvell was captured.

Copp continues his criticism of Stacey in his concluding chapter "Normandy: A New Balance Sheet."[413] The Allied campaign in Normandy resulted in one of the greatest military victories in modern history. This extraordinary achievement has failed to impress military historians, who have developed an interpretation of the campaign that emphasizes operational and tactical failure.[414] The Germans had a series of costly defeats against the 7th Brigade; however, the one temporary success at Putot-en Bessin provides the basis for describing the German force as superior even though the Canadians had won numerous battles against them. The efforts of the Canadians showed the fearlessness and determination they possessed and I believe that historians should not view them as failures.

The Canadian failure to push forward between 7 and 10 June is simply part of the larger narrative of the failure of the I British Corps in front of Caen. Marc Milner sets out to counter this narrative in his book *Stopping the Panzers: The Untold Story of D-Day* (2014). Milner contends that the Canadians were to take and hold the only ground on which the planners believed that an attack on the Allied landings in Normandy could be decisive. Their job was to stop the panzers.[415] He argues that Stacey and his team of Canadian Army official historians never knew the ultimate purposes of the Canadian assault on D-Day and the battles ashore between 7 and 10 June. The "failure to move forward paradigm" has dominated the Normandy story since Stacey did not know the ultimate purpose and argued that the Canadians were stopped. Milner also contents that it was not until Terry Copp published his book *Fields of Fire* that the account of the Canadian experience in Normandy changed. Milner continues with this new narrative of the Canadians in Normandy.

The Canadians succeeded in stopping the German counterattacks on D+2 to D+4. The bridgehead battles showed the strength and courage of the Canadians. For the Royal Winnipeg Rifles, the Battle of Putot-en-Bessin almost completely destroyed the regiment, but their task was accomplished. Milner describes this battle in detail, arguing that the town appeared to be a good, defensible location. However, once the Winnipegs arrived, they quickly saw that they were at a disadvantage. While Lieutenant Colonel J. M. Meldram had been criticized for his placement of the Winnipegs around the town, he asserts that the British would be there to help cover the open flank.[416] Communication was a key problem in this battle, from the 7th Brigade not knowing the British movements to the Winnipegs not advising headquarters that they were losing the battle until the Germans had taken the town for numerous hours. Even though with the Winnipegs lost the town, they were still able to keep the Germans from pressing forward with their counterattack and ultimately stopped their counterattack. Milner's main premise is that the Canadians' Operation Overlord task was to stop the panzers and they achieved that task.[417]

The Normandy invasion was just another battle in the long history of the Royal Winnipeg Rifles. This regiment has a history of always being ready for battle and one who would not shy away from danger. Brian A. Reid's *Named by the Enemy: A History of the Royal Winnipeg Rifles* (2010) is an updated version of the official regimental history of the Winnipegs. Reid uses firsthand accounts, the war diaries, and published sources to write a detailed history of the regiment, adding in the firsthand accounts and published sources to the war diaries help to elaborate on the information found in the diaries. When the Second World War broke out, the Winnipegs quickly began recruiting and went overseas. They spent close to four years training before going into battle. The Winnipegs displayed great courage during Operation Overlord and the Battle of Putot-en-Bessin. Reid describes the landing, the push inland, and the battle at Putot in great detail. He agrees with Milner's premise that the Winnipegs were able to stop the German counter even in their defeat. Putot was a tactical defeat; however, it was a strategic victory that stalled the enemy's advance at a critical juncture.[418]

The firsthand accounts on the Normandy invasion are significant sources to examine as I pieced together my great-great uncle's story. Ted Barris's *Juno: Canadians at D-Day, June 6, 1944* (2004), is a more personal account of the Canadians during this initial invasion than those of Stacey, Milner, or Copp. He uses personal accounts and letters to humanize the tale. The focus of the book is not strictly about the army, but rather all sections of the military that held Canadians. Through adding of the different sections of the military, Barris provides readers with a rounded account of the events and the amount of work that was needed to make this mission a success. Barris begins the book with a discussion of the Dieppe Raid and how the Allied nations used this to plan the Normandy invasion. The Allies needed to work from the same battle plan and purpose for this invasion to succeed.[419]

Barris spends the majority of the book focusing on the initial invasion on 6 June. Two brothers, who were in the Royal Winnipeg Rifles, described their fears in letters to their mother before going into this battle. Many of the Winnipegs were told that they would not be going back home after this.[420] This presents the reader with the realities that the Canadian soldiers had to endure before and after the invasion. Barris also includes a chapter on the days following D-Day when the Canadians fought the 12th SS Panzer Division and other elite German forces.

While Barris uses firsthand accounts to add in the personal connection to the Normandy invasion and subsequent battles, Jean Portugal's series *We Were There* (1998) contains only firsthand accounts from the soldiers of the Second World War. In volume 6, Portugal focuses on the Winnipegs and their participation in the Normandy invasion, the battle of Putot-en-Bessin, and the liberation of Europe. The detailed accounts from their soldiers provide the human connection that is often left out or minimized in the literature which is one reason why I wrote this book. It also provides a shared experience to that of Carvell. The experiences that the soldiers described each became part of the collective memory of the Winnipegs during this campaign. While the personal accounts are important to have, these accounts were given many years after the war. Every one of the soldiers stated that there were certain memories that he could not recall even after all the years. Memories can change and fade over time; however, these accounts cannot be discredited. The Normandy landings and the battle of Putot-en-Bessin remained in the minds of these men as many described these experiences in detail even years after the fact.

The battle of Putot-en-Bessin was significant for the Royal Winnipeg Rifles. Their orders were simple: hold their position and stop any German assault. Mike Bechthold's chapter in

Canada and the Second World War entitled "Defending the Normandy Bridgehead: The Battles for Putot-en Bessin, 7-9 June 1944," (2012) describes, in detail, the effort of the Winnipegs and the contributions of the Canadian Scottish Regiment. Bechthold builds on the same approach that Copp employs by reconstructing the battle using message logs and war diaries. He argues that the Germans failure to capture and hold Putot was the direct result of the prolonged resistance by the Rifles and the timely and effective 7th Brigade counterattack.[421]

English was a harsh critic of the Winnipegs' performance during this battle, stating that three German companies put the three Canadian companies to flight.[422] According to Bechthold's research, the Germans had deployed more than three companies of infantry; they had three assault companies and a fourth heavy weapons company.[423] Milner points out that the strength of 12th SS companies was double that of Canadian companies. This counters English's argument that it was only three companies that fought. The importance of the Winnipegs' action on 8 June cannot be overstated. A complete collapse would have had dire consequences for the Regina's position at Bretteville-Norrey and perhaps for the Allied beachhead.[424]

The Battle of Putot-en-Bessin was costly for the 7th Brigade; however, it also showed the professionalism and skill of the Canadian Army in Normandy. The Winnipegs' lost 256 men including 150 men captured.[425] The Canadian Scottish Regiment suffered125 casualties, including 45 men killed in action. This was a costly victory for the 7th Brigade but it was a victory that was a result of tactical skill rather than brute force. It also showed the skill of the Canadian commanders and their troops.[426]

The literature on the prisoners of war in Normandy is relativity limited compared to the extensive amount of literature on the battle campaign. The majority of Canadian prisoner of war research is on the Dieppe prisoners and those captured in Hong Kong by the Japanese. These prisoners of war had very different experiences in captivity. Daniel Dancocks's *In Enemy Hands* (1983) is a popular history; however, it still is a useful beginning for studying the subject of Canadian prisoners of war. The book provides firsthand accounts from members of the army, air force, and navy who were all captured during different periods of the war. Dancocks argues that Canadian prisoners of war are the forgotten men of World War II.[427] He believes that most of the literature of the Second World War glosses over or completely leaves out the plight of the POWs. This is a stark contrast to the United States and Britain which both have significant literature on the subject.

Dancocks provides accounts of prisoners from all the theatres of the war. This enables the reader to compare the different experiences of prisoners. Even the prisoners who were captured by the Germans near the beginning of the war had very different experiences than those who were captured after the Normandy assault. Dancocks describes how the collapse of Germany was both good and bad news for prisoners. They could look forward to liberation but the conditions in the prison camps began to deteriorate.[428] While the prisoners were no longer fighting on the battlefield, they were now fighting for their lives. This fight is a significant story that needs to be explored far beyond what scholars have already done.

While Dancocks describes prisoners of war as the "forgotten men," Jonathan Vance believes this to be misleading. He argues that POWs were frequently misunderstood and occasionally subordinated to larger political objective, but they were rarely forgotten.[429] Vance's *Objects of Concern: Canadian Prisoners of War Through the Twentieth Century* (1994) examines the treatment of POWs through both world wars, the effort made at home, and the reintegration of ex-POWs into society. While Vance does not examine the Normandy POWs in great detail, his book still provides an excellent overview on the general experiences of the soldiers. Early in his examination of the Second World War, Vance points out that the armed forces rarely considered the possibility of capture and most servicemen never contemplated that they might fall into enemy hands.[430] Training was lacking in this area. While this preparation training was needed, it was often left out of the programs, which led soldiers to rely on their own basic instincts for survival. However, after the murders of Canadian soldiers by the 12th SS Panzer Division in Normandy, commanders quickly realized that they needed to start preparing their soldiers for this possibility. Vance provides a general description of what the prison camps were like and the numerous survival techniques that were employed. Food was always an issue for POWs. Carvell often spoke about the lack of sweets and cigarettes in his letters home; however, it was not until he filled his war claims form that he fully acknowledged the scarcity of food. Near the end of the war, food packages from the Red Cross could not get to the camps.

Once the war was over and the POWs were liberated, the soldiers were faced with reintegration into society. This is an important theme in Vance's book. He describes how the reintegration into society would not be easy for all ex-prisoners.[431] The government worked hard to help these men. However, the medical treatment and counselling that some ex-prisoners needed and that so many of the war time reports had stressed was almost non-existent.[432] Carvell's reintegration into society, for example, appears to be relatively smooth compared to others who had similar experiences. However, his time spent as a POW followed him through his life.

The prisoners of war in Normandy who were murdered by the 12th SS Panzer Division are often the focus of the literature on POWs. Howard Margolian's *Conduct Unbecoming: The Story of the Murder of Canadian Prisoners of War in Normandy* (1998) provides a detailed account of what happened to the 156 soldiers who were murdered. Margolian states that he wrote the book for two reasons. The first was a warning of what can happen when soldiers are dehumanized by political indoctrination, the encouragement of ugly prejudices, and the creed of blind obedience. The second purpose is to honour oft-forgotten and occasionally scorned heroes.[433] He presents a thorough description of the 12th SS Panzer Division and the doctrine that they followed. This grants the reader the ability to examine how these youth were able to commit these murders.

The Canadians who met their deaths from this group preserved, for all time, that which their killers had tried to erase with cowardly murders and unmarked graves—their essential humanity.[434] Margolian presents accounts of the prisoners last moments. A number of these moments will never be fully known, as the only people who know what happened were also killed. Forensic evidence was used to reconstruct these final minutes.[435] Each of the accounts, whether based on eye witnesses or reconstruction, exhibited the courage of the Canadians during these inhumane times. While these prisoners showed great courage this was not the "normal" POW experience for the Canadians who were captured during this time period.

Major Jack Veness and Major Jack Fairweather had significantly different POW experiences than those described by Margolian. One could even say that these men had what was called the "normal" POW experience while they were in captivity. Will R. Bird provides a detailed account of the experiences of Veness and Fairweather in *Two Jacks: The Amazing Adventures of Major Jack M. Veness and Major Jack L. Fairweather* (1955). Both Veness and Fairweather were with the North Nova Scotia Highlanders (North Novas), part of the 9 Canadian Infantry Brigade during the Normandy invasions. Bird provides a detailed description of the initial landings of the North Novas on Juno Beach and their push inland. Veness and Fairweather's experiences were different from Carvell's due largely to the fact that 9 Brigade was in the second wave of regiments landing after 7 and 8 Brigades cleared the beaches. Even they faced enemy fire on D-Day; however, not to the extent that Carvell and the Winnipegs endured.

While the Normandy landings contributed to different experiences for Carvell, Veness, and Fairweather, their capture by the 12th SS Division during the subsequent beachhead battles were similar in nature. Veness and Fairweather were captured during the Battle of Authie on 7 June 1944. They were marched to the Abbeye d'Ardenne before being moved to a POW camp.[436] While Veness and Fairweather were on a different march, they were still confronted with similar hardships as Carvell—lack of food, danger, and exhaustion. They were all placed in the Rennes prison camp. Bird presents a comprehensive description of the camp and what life was like.

This account is significant because there is limited literature on the camps in which the Normandy POWs were initially placed, and this provides a better understanding of Carvell's first camp experience. Carvell was unable to describe the camp in his letter home;[437] therefore, having this account fills in some of the blanks that are not found in his letters. Veness and Fairweather were officers so their duties in the camp were different than Carvell's, but this does not detract from the significance of the account. One of the substantial differences between Carvell and Veness and Fairweather is that the two officers escaped while they were being transported into Germany. Bird continues their account of their escape, their participation in the French underground, and their homecoming. Veness and Fairweather's experiences in the war were an amazing adventure, the stuff of movies.

The Normandy POW experience was vastly different from those captured at Hong Kong. The Canadian government never wanted to send troops to Hong Kong because of the imperial connotations that were present. Hong Kong was a British Crown colony and Canada was hesitant to send soldiers to protect British imperialism. However, after pressure from Britain, Canada sent two battalions for garrison duty in late 1941.[438] The Royal Rifles of Canada and the Winnipeg Grenadiers were chosen for this post.[439] The Canadian soldiers were a part of a largely British and Indian garrison. They were told that the Japanese were ill equipped, unused to night fighting, and only totalled about 5000 men, therefore, they would not be a threat to the men. The Japanese attacked the Canadian position on 18 December 1941. By Christmas, the Canadians and British had surrendered and for almost the next four years, the survivors of this surrender had to survive being POWs in a nation that rejected the Geneva Convention and viewed soldiers who surrendered as cowards.[440] This left the governments of the POWs anxious about what the Japanese would do to their POWs.

The Canadians captured in Hong Kong endured unspeakable horrors that no other Canadian POWs experienced. Charles G Roland's book *Long Night's Journey into Night: Prisoners of War in Hong Kong and Japan, 1941-1945* (2001) describes the treatment and means of survival that the men found. Roland argues that it did not matter where the men were captured; being a POW of the Japanese was a frightening experience and often led to the possibility of being shot on the spot.[441] Since the Japanese ignored the Geneva Convention, their treatment methods and camps were significantly different from the west. While the Canadians were not summarily executed like the Normandy POWs, the Hong Kong POWs had a difficult time surviving because of the lack of food and the diseases that ran through the camps. Many of these diseases were preventable and curable. However, the Japanese refused to have proper facilities for the men and would not obtain the proper medicine once it ran out. The Japanese also refused to give the POWs the packages that the Red Cross sent containing food and other items.

Roland contends that there was one element of prisoner life that stood out: the brutality that the Canadians endured on a daily basis. Escaping was nearly impossible, and those who tried and failed were made into examples. However, while there was brutality, there were also pleasant events. They did receive some mail,[442] those were happy events. Sports were a pastime the men enjoyed, when they were not too sick to participate. Since escaping was almost impossible, the men found other ways to help the war effort through sabotage. Any minor successful sabotage gave the men joy and hope.[443] The men who came home after spending almost four years in captivity did so because of their survival skills, their ability to adapt to their environment, and a measure of simple luck. The men did their best to look out for one another and kept each other alive.

Dieppe POWs had a significantly different experience than the men in Hong Kong; however, there were some similarities in their need for survival and morale. The Dieppe Raid of 1942 was a tactical failure and the casualties were heavy. There are an abundance of memoirs and books on the Dieppe Raid and the POW experience. Jack A Poolton's memoir *Destined to Survive: A Dieppe Veteran's Story* (1998) describes his battle and captivity experiences. He was with the Royal Regiment of Canada, which landed on Puys Beach and was the last to surrender when the raid failed. One significant statement that Poolton writes about his capture was, "you can train a soldier to fight and you can train a soldier to accept death, but there is no way to prepare a soldier to be taken prisoner."[444] This is a common theme among POWs especially those captured at Dieppe. Survival is another main theme of Poolton's text.

Poolton's experiences in the POW camps were in great contrast to those who were captured in Hong Kong. While there was still some mistreatment, the Germans were not as brutal as the Japanese. The Red Cross packages kept the men alive. One of the most difficult parts of Poolton's captivity was when the Germans bound the hands of all the prisoners.[445] They spent 410 days bound. However, this did not stop the men from continuing their war effort. Death marches at the end of the war in the winter of 1945 provided some of the worst conditions for the POWs. The Normandy POWs experienced these marches as well as the war was nearing its end.

A. Robert Prouse had similar experiences as Poolton when he was captured at Dieppe. His memoir *Ticket to Hell via Dieppe* (1982) describes his experiences in the POW hospital, camps, and trying to escape. Treatment changed depending on the camp the men were in. Some camps were overcrowded and unable to handle the amount of prisoners that were being sent there. Even with the lack of food, overcrowding, and long work days, the Dieppe POWs were still about to find ways to keep morale lifted and make the best of the situation. Prouse described that, "the things that made it possible to endure were the comradeship and unselfishness of most prisoners, along with humour of daily happenings."[446] These men could survive any situation and make the best of the situation until they were free again. All the different POWs found ways to keep their morale up and be positive even when they were not in the most ideal situations.

Being in battle and captivity changed many lives during the war. The men learned how to survive by any means necessary, even in ways they could never have previously imagined. Once the war was over soldiers had to reintegrate into society. This was not always an easy thing to do. Many veterans came home with battle exhaustion, and they did not have the support that they needed to continue with their lives. Carvell was able to reintegrate within society relatively easily. However, he still had to cope with the battle exhaustion. His captivity had a profound effect on his life, but he used those experiences to keep going. Terry Copp and Bill McAndrew's book *Battle Exhaustion: Soldiers and Psychiatrics in the Canadian Army, 1939-1945* (1990) examines battle exhaustion through the war and measures that were used to combat this problem. Battle exhaustion was the new term used instead of shell shock which was used in the First World War, and what we now call Post Traumatic Stress Disorder (PTSD). After the First World War, medical and military professionals needed more help to cope with the psychiatric casualties and to understand how to combat the condition if another war broke out. Copp and McAndrew seek to explain the types of situations that soldiers found themselves in that led to battle exhaustion.[447] They argue that modern armies assume that anxiety states are inseparable from battle, and will rise and fall in relation to such factors as morale and intensity of combat. The current wisdom is that such casualties can be quickly returned to duty if frontline treatment based on the principles of proximity, immediacy, and expectancy is available.[448]

Not every soldier who went into war suffered from crippling battle exhaustion. There were varying degrees of it and the success of treatment varied from soldier to soldier. Copp and McAndrew argue that each soldier entering a battle carries within himself a varying degree of predisposition or vulnerability to combat stress, which may or may not lead to breakdown, depending on numerous factors, not excluding the fortunes of war.[449] Morale and motivation, as well as luck and timing, were largely immeasurable factors in sustaining soldiers. Individual, situational, and organizational factors all played a part in determining an individual's breaking point.[450] Each soldier could sustain a certain amount of trauma (combat or captivity) before reaching their breaking point. Once the soldier reached that breaking point, they needed to have support in place to help them either get back into battle or be able to function in society. Carvell recognized that he suffered from this after the war and needed help to cope properly.

With the literature on the Normandy invasion so vast, one questions whether anything new can be discussed. The training of the army before the invasion is often heavily criticized. Training a citizen army was no easy task and should not be so strongly criticized. Using the regimental war diaries and personal accounts of Carvell and others will help establish a better understanding of the training that the army used. New approaches are bringing to light the professionalism of the Canadian army. Once in battle, the initial invasion and following days were significant for the Royal Winnipeg Rifles. The courage and professionalism is shown during the fighting and when many were captured by the Germans. The treatment of POWs captured in Normandy (those who were not murdered), is poorly documented. *The Two Jacks* is one of the few books that describes the experiences of the Normandy POWs and provides insight into the first camp in which Carvell was placed. Carvell spent eleven months travelling from France to what is now Czech Republic, where he was liberated. The numerous camps he was placed in and the work he was forced to do provide an important piece of history that is not easily found. Even though soldiers were captured and placed in different environments, there were many similarities to their experiences. These men put all the effort into surviving and helping the war effort any way possible. Most POWs felt guilty for being captured; therefore, escaping and sabotaging became popular pastimes for the men. This helped to alleviate some of the guilt. POWs and returning soldiers faced numerous challenges when coming back home and reintegrating back into society. While many returning soldiers suffered battle exhaustion, Carvell came home and reintegrated into society with little or no problems. He used his war experiences as a means for educating others, and he lived a full life.

ACKNOWLEDGEMENTS

There are so many people that I would like to thank for all their help and support through this project. First would be Dr. Marc Milner. I could not have asked for a better supervisor for this project and I am truly lucky to have his guidance and knowledge. He brought my researching, writing, and historical thought to another level. He also introduced me to the concept of walking the battlefields to fully understand them. I am grateful that I had him during those emotional moments in Europe.

To The Gregg Centre for the Study of War and Society who provided me with constant guidance and resources that were essential for this project. I am grateful for meeting so many wonderful people within this centre. I am also grateful for the History Department at the University of New Brunswick, whose professors were so willing to help when needed.

Thank you to the archivists at Library and Archives Canada for all your help during my initial archive search. You made using the archives so much easier for a first time visitor.

Thank you to my publisher Jeremy Lammi of Lammi Publishing Inc. You have been very easy to work with and appreciate all the support when life would get in the way of getting the edits done. Thank you to my editor Karen Hann. You've really helped bring this book to life in so many different ways. I appreciate all the support during this process.

This project never would have occurred had it not been for Sandra Crawford, Uncle George's daughter. Sandra willing gave me all of her father's records, letters, newspapers, and answered any questions I had. I am forever grateful for all of her help.

I especially would like to thank my parents, Bob and Elizabeth Shepherd, for their constant encouragement and support throughout this project. I could not have done it without them.

My husband, Adam, has been my cheerleader during this whole process of turning my thesis into a book. He has supported me during all the hours of going back to my research, listening to all the new things I learned, and giving me the encouragement needed when my motivation disappeared. Thank you.

Lastly, to all my family, friends, and colleagues thank you for your help and kind words. It means more than I can ever describe.

Amanda Shepherd

07/16/2018

St. Albert, Alberta

End Notes

1 Tim Cook, *The Necessary War: Canadians Fighting the Second World War, 1939-1943,Vol. I,* (Toronto: The Penguin Group, 2014), 23

2 Brian Reid, *Named by the Enemy: A History of the Royal Winnipeg Rifles*, (Altona, Manitoba: Robin Brass Studio, Inc, 2010), 166.

3 Both Stacey and English are highly critical of the Winnipegs for their showing at this battle and blame the reinforcements and officers for this poor showing.

4 E.R. Fobes, "The 1930s: The Depression and Retrenchment," E.R. Fobes eds. *The Atlantic Provinces in Confederation* (Toronto: University of Toronto Press, 1993), 274. For providing direct relief, the cost was shared on a one-third, one-third, one-third basis, but the municipality had to come up with the first third and administrate the program. Most were unable to do so.

5 Author's personal collection, George Carvell's service file.

6 Barris, *Juno*, 111.

7 Popular history focuses more on the narrative and vivid, personal accounts of history than scholarly analysis. Often these histories are written by journalists.

8 Daniel G. Dancocks, *In Enemy Hands: Canadian Prisoners of War, 1939*-45, (Edmonton: Hurtig Publishers, 1983), ix.

9 Howard Margolian, *Conduct Unbecoming: The Story of the Murder of Canadian Prisoners of War in Normandy*, (Toronto: University of Toronto Press, 1998), ix. The book was the first to capture this dark moment in detail. Recent scholarship has added to the literature on this topic.

10 Veness and Fairweather were placed in a barn in the Abbeye while Myer's men were killing the Canadian prisoners in the garden. Will R

Bird, *The Two Jacks: The Amazing Adventures of Major Jack M. Veness and Major Jack L. Fairweather*, (Philadelphia, Macrae Smith, 1955), 21.

11 Carvell's only letter from this camp appears to be scripted. Veness wrote the same letter home when he arrived at the camp. Bird, *The Two Jacks*, 119.

12 Jack Poolton, *Destined to Survive: A Dieppe Veteran's Story*, (Toronto: Dundurn Press, 1998), 41.

13 Tim Cook, *The Necessary War*, 22.

14 Howard Graham, *Citizen and Soldier: The Memoirs of Lieutenant General Howard Graham*. (Toronto: McClelland and Stewart, 1987), 109.

15 Tom Didmon. *Lucky Guy: Memoirs of a World War II Canadian Soldier.* Victoria: Trafford Publishing, 2000, 2.

16 Jonathan Vance, *Maple Leaf Empire: Canada, Britain, and Two World Wars*, (Toronto: OUP Canada, 2012), 150. Some of the other reasons that men enlisted were to escape—wives, families, obligations and imperial sentiments. With this war, men had to make the rational choice of enlisting or waiting until conscription transpired again.

17 Cook, *The Necessary War*, 26-27.

18 Stacey, *Six Years of War*, 113.

19 Cook, *The Necessary War*, 27.

20 Stacey, *Six Years of War*, 113.

21 Copp and McAndrew, *Battle Exhaustion*, 13.

22 Copp and McAndrew, *Battle Exhaustion*, 12.

23 C.P. Stacey and Barbara M. Wilson, *The Half Million: The Canadians in Britain, 1939-1946*, (Toronto: University of Toronto Press, 1987), 3.

24 Copp, *Fields of Fire*, 15.

25 Donald Ripley, *The Home Front: Wartime Life in Camp Aldershot and Kentville, Nova Scotia*, (Hantsport: Lancelot Press, 1992), p. 11.

26 Stacey, *Six Years of War*, 142.

27 Author's personal collection, Carvell's service record.

[28] English, *The Canadian Army*, 75.

[29] Historical Section of the General Staff, *The Canadian in Britain, 1939-44*, (Ottawa: The King's Printer, 1944), 50.

[30] Stacey, *Six Years of War*, 133.

[31] Vance, *Maple Leaf Empire,* 151.

[32] Library and Archives Canada (LAC), Record Group (RG) 24, Vol. 16,749, 1st Canadian Division Infantry Reinforcement Unit war diary, July 1942, appendix 2

[33] Stacey, *Six Years War,* 234.

[34] Stacey, *Six Years War,* 238.

[35] C. P. Stacey, *The Canadian Army 1939-1945*, (Ottawa: King's Printer, 1948), 31.

[36] Stacey, *Six Years War,* 239.

[37] Stacey, *Six Years War,* 239.

[38] Ibid. 240.

[39] LAC, RG 24, Vol. 16,749, 1st Canadian Division Infantry Reinforcement Unit war diary, July 1942, appendix 2.

[40] LAC, RG 24, Vol. 16,749, 1st Canadian Division Infantry Reinforcement Unit war diary, July 1942, appendix 1.

[41] English, *The Canadian Army*, 114.

[42] MacDonald, "The Long Wait (Part1)," 40.

[43] English, *The Canadian Army*, 114.

[44] Copp, *Fires of* Fire, 18.

[45] English, *The Canadian Army*, 115. Farley Mowat described, in his memoir *And No Bird Sang*, that he was able to identify the majority of German weapons by sound and this helped him understand the battle situation significantly better and he could tell his soldiers what to expect. Farley Mowat, *And No Bird Sang*, (Toronto: McCelland and Stewart, 1979), 95.

[46] Author's personal collection, Carvell's service file.

[47] Stacey, *Six Years War*, 133.

[48] Ibid. 133.

[49] Stacey, *Six Years War*, 203.

[50] Ibid. 206.

[51] LAC, RG 24, Vol. 16,749, No. 2 "Wolf" Battalion War Diary, May 1942.

[52] LAC, RG 24, Vol. 15,233, 7th Canadian Infantry Reinforcement Unit War Diary, March 1943.

[53] If Carvell would have stayed with the 1 C.D.I.R.U., he would have been sent to Sicily with the 1st Canadian Division when they went in July 1943.

[54] LAC, RG 24, Vol. 15,233, 7th Canadian Infantry Reinforcement Unit War Diary, February 1943.

[55] LAC, RG 24, Vol. 15,233, 7th Canadian Infantry Reinforcement Unit War Diary, September 1943. There is no clear indication in the war diaries whether the 7 C.I.R.U was attached to the 7th Canadian Infantry Brigade even though they did have members of the 7th Brigade in the reinforcement unit.

[56] George Edward Meakin, of the Royal Winnipeg Rifles, spent from November 7, 1941 until December 27, 1941 in the 3rd Canadian Division Infantry Reinforcement Unit after being in the hospital before he was placed back with the regiment. LAC, RG 24, Vol. 26,595, George Edward Meakin's service file.

[57] The 7th C.I.R.U. participated in an exercise to defend two of the training camps from enemy attack. LAC, RG 24, Vol. 15,233, 7th Canadian Infantry Reinforcement Unit War Diary, October 1943, Appendix 4.

[58] Monica Inman, "'Hugs...Tears' As NB Veteran Relives D-Day," *The Victory County Record*, 10 November 1994, 12.

[59] Author's personal collection, Carvell's service file.

[60] Inman, "'Hugs...Tears' As NB Veteran Relives D-Day, 12.

[61] Vance, *Maple Leaf Empire*, 178.

[62] Vance, *Maple Leaf Empire*, p. 170.

[63] Stacey and Wilson, *The Half Million*, 96.

[64] Mark Maclay, *Aldershot's Canadians: In Love and War 1939-45*, (Farnborough, Applin, 1997), 90.

[65] LAC, RG 24, Vol. 16,749, 1st Canadian Infantry Division Reinforcement Unit War Diary, July 1942.

[66] The war diaries for the reinforcement units document these sport days and the outcomes. This demonstrated how important these competitions were among the soldiers and units.

[67] Stacey and Wilson, *The Half Million*, 96.

[68] Stacey and Wilson, *The Half Million*, 98.

[69] 7th Canadian Infantry Reinforcement Unit war diary describes weekly film nights for the soldiers and lists each other the different films that were being shown through the month. LAC, RG 24, Vol. 15,233, 7th Canadian Infantry Reinforcement Unit war diary, May, 1943.

[70] LAC, RG 24, Vol. 16, 749, 1st Canadian Division Infantry Reinforcement Unit, War Diary, July 1942. A group of officers and men went to see a house dance at one of the lady's homes.

[71] Maclay, *Aldershot's Canadians*, 85.

[72] George Carvell to Mrs. Otis Kierstead, 8 June 1943, Author's personal collection.

[73] Carvell sent his niece a hanky in one of his letters to his sister. Ibid.

[74] Stacey and Wilson, *The Half Million*, 119.

[75] Carvell and Smith were friends in Plaster Rock, New Brunswick. Smith died of wounds in July, 1944.

[76] George Carvell to Mrs. Otis Kierstead, 8 June 1943, Author's personal collection.

[77] LAC, RG 24, Vol. 27,084, William W. Smith's service file.

[78] 48,000 Canadians married during the course of the war, with about 94 percent of the brides being British. Cook, *Fight to the Finish,* 412-13.

[79] Maclay, *Aldershot's Canadians,* 97-113.

[80] Maclay, *Aldershot's Canadians,* 117.

[81] Carvell had tried to reconnect with Pullinger when he went to Britain during the 50th anniversary of D-Day tour. He was unable to reconnect.

[82] Maclay, *Aldershot's Canadians,* 121.

[83] Stacey and Wilson, *The Half Million,* 136. Later the regulations changed to the soldiers had to declare their marital status and women needed character references before they could marry.

[84] Vance, *Maple Leaf Empire,* 177.

[85] Ibid. 178.

[86] Author's personal collection, Carvell's service file.

[87] Maclay, *Aldershot's Canadians,* 135.

[88] Stacey and Wilson, *The Half Million,* 159.

[89] Stacey, *Six Years of War,* 330.

[90] See David O'Keefe's work *One Day in August: The Untold Story Behind Canada's Tragedy at Dieppe,* (Toronto: Knopf Canada, 2013).

[91] Cook, *The Necessary War,* 254.

[92] Granatstein, *The Best Little Army in the World: The Canadians Fighting in Northwest Europe 1944-1945,* (Toronto: HarperCollins, 2015), 27.

[93] Maclay, *Aldershot's Canadians,* 169.

[94] Granatstein, *The Best Little Army in the World,* 27.

[95] Cook, *The Necessary War,* 258.

[96] Granatstein, *The Best Little Army in the World,* 28, Cook, *The Necessary War,* 261.

[97] I spent some time at Puys Beach during my Canadian Battlefields Study Tour. It is difficult to describe the beach until you have set foot

on it. Trying to walk and run up the beach in sneakers was extremely difficult. It was difficult to imagine what the soldier would have endured trying to get on that beach with the Germans higher positions.

[98] Stacey, *Six Years of War*, 363.

[99] Stacey, *Six Years of War*, 366, Cook, *The Necessary War*, 265.

[100] Cook, *The Necessary War*, 265.

[101] Stacey, *Six Years of War*, 368, Cook, *The Necessary War*, 266-267, Granatstein, *The Best Little Army in the World*, 28.

[102] O'Keefe, *One Day in August*, 357.

[103] Cook, *The Necessary War*, 269-270, Stacey, *Six Years of War*, 272.

[104] Mark Zuehlke, *Tragedy at Dieppe: Operation Jubilee, August 19, 1942*, (Toronto: Douglas& McIntyre, 2012), 275.

[105] Cook, *The Necessary War*, 272.

[106] Cook, *The Necessary War*, 277.

[107] Cook, *The Necessary War*, 278, Stacey, *Six Years of War*, 386.

[108] Maclay, *Aldershot's Canadians*, 171.

[109] Milner, *Stopping the Panzers*, 35.

[110] Milner, *Stopping the Panzers*, 50.

[111] Stacey, *The Victory Campaign*, 17.

[112] Cook, *Fight to the Finish*, 97.

[113] Milner, *Stopping the Panzers*, 82.

[114] Milner, *Stopping the Panzers*, 64.

[115] The 1st Canadian Infantry Division was sent to Italy in 1943. The government wanted the division back by 1944; however, they continued their campaign in Italy.

[116] Cook, *Fight to the Finish*, 114.

[117] Milner, *Stopping the Panzers*, 64.

[118] Milner, *Stopping the Panzers*, 65.

[119] Milner, *Stopping the Panzers*, 66.

[120] Cook, *Fight to the Finish*, 115.

[121] Stacey, *The Victory Campaign*, 35-36.

[122] Reid, *Named by the Enemy, 150.*

[123] LAC, RG 24, Vol. 15233, Royal Winnipeg Rifles war diary, January 1944.

[124] Reid, *Named by the Enemy,* 151.

[125] LAC, RG 24, Vol. 15233, Royal Winnipeg Rifles war diary, January 1944.

[126] LAC, RG 24, Vol. 15233, Royal Winnipeg Rifles war diary, February 1944.

[127] Exercise Trousers was the first rehearsal based on the Operation Overlord plan. It was the first time the Canadians were able to practice landing in a uniform fashion. Margolion, *Conduct Unbecoming,* 17.

[128] There was no mention in the war dairies of any training for the soldiers on if they were captured during the invasion. There were two lectures that month on how to treat POWs. LAC, RG 24, Vol. 15233, Royal Winnipeg Rifles war diary, April 1944.

[129] LAC, RG 24, Vol. 15233, Royal Winnipeg Rifles war diary, April 1944.

[130] LAC, RG 24, Vol. 15233, Royal Winnipeg Rifles war diary, April 1944.

[131] Reid, *Named by the Enemy,* 151.

[132] Fabius produced valuable results, particularly in the practice it afforded in the marshalling, embarkation and sailing of the assault forces. Stacey, *The Victory Campaign*, p. 37.

[133] Reid, *Named by the Enemy,* 152.

[134] LAC, RG 24, Vol. 15233, Royal Winnipeg Rifles war diary, Battle Notes No. 1, May, 1944.

[135] LAC, RG 24, Vol. 15233, Royal Winnipeg Rifles war diary, June, 1944.

[136] Vance, *Maple Leaf Empire*, p. 204.

[137] Jean E. Portugal, *We Were There: The Army, A Record for Canada*, vol. 6, (Toronto: Royal Canadian Military Institute Heritage Society, 1998), 2875.

[138] Portugal, *We Were There,* 2888. L-Cpl John W. McLean stated that he wrote to his wife and parents and neither received the letters. Many other soldiers who were interviewed after the war asked their loved ones about these letters and received the same information, they were never received.

[139] LAC, RG 24, Vol. 15,233, Royal Winnipeg Rifles, War Diary, 5 June 1944.

[140] Portugal, *We Were There,* 2888.

[141] Copp, *Fields of* Fire, 40-41.

[142] This goes against the narrative that the air power attack was the decisive victory in the Normandy invasion.

[143] Cook, *Fight to the Finish*, 126.

[144] Milner, *Stopping the Panzers*, 194.

[145] Ibid, 114.

[146] LAC, RG 24, Vol.15168, War Diary of 1 Bn. The Queen's Own Rifles of Canada, 6 June 1944.

[147] Cook, *Fight to the Finish*, 128, Granstain, *The Best Little Army*, 73.

[148] Milner, *Stopping the Panzers*, 114.

[149] Stacey, *The Victory Campaign,* 108.

[150] LAC, RG 24, Vol.15168, War Diary of 1 Bn. The Queen's Own Rifles of Canada, 6 June 1944.

[151] LAC, RG 24, Vol.15168, War Diary of 1 Bn. The Queen's Own Rifles of Canada, 6 June 1944.

[152] LAC, RG 24, Vol. 15127, The War Diary of the North Shore (New Brunswick) Regiment, 6 June 1944.

153 It took most of the morning for B Company and the tanks to destroy the strong point. Forty-eight prisoners were taken during this time. LAC, RG 24, Vol. 15127, The War Diary of the North Shore (New Brunswick) Regiment, 6 June 1944.

154 Milner, *Stopping the Panzers,*115.

155 Stacey, *The Victory Campaign*, 109, Milner, *Stopping the Panzers,*117.

156 LAC, RG 24, Vol. 15,233, Royal Winnipeg Rifles, War Diary, 6 June 1944.

157 LAC, RG 24, Vol. 15,233, Royal Winnipeg Rifles, War Diary, 6 June 1944.

158 Stacey, *The Victory Campaign,* 103.

159 Milner, *Stopping the Panzers,* 195.

160 Stacey, *The Victory Campaign,* 104.

161 Barris, *Juno*, 110. Major Fulton stated that it was hard to describe the difficulty in getting through the sea water and across the beach to the relative safety of the sand dunes, with your battledress full of water and carrying a heavy load of ammunition and equipment. Portugal, *We Were There*, 2916.

162 Portugal, *We Were There,* 3054.

163 Ibid. 2875.

164 Stacey, *The Victory Campaign,* 104.

165 Bruce Tascna, Eric Wells, *The Little Black Devils: A History of the Royal Winnipeg Rifles,*(Manitoba: Frye Publishing, 1983), 146.

166 LAC, RG 24, Vol. 15,233, Royal Winnipeg Rifles, War Diary, 6 June 1944.

167 Portugal, *We Were There,* 3032.

168 LAC, RG 24, Vol. 15,233, Royal Winnipeg Rifles, War Diary, June 1944, Appendix 6.

169 LAC, RG 24, Vol. 15,233, Royal Winnipeg Rifles, War Diary, June 1944, Appendix 6.

[170] Inman, "'Hugs…Tears' As NB Veteran Relives D-Day," 12.

[171] Portugal, *We Were There,* 2917.

[172] LAC, RG 24, Vol. 15,233, Royal Winnipeg Rifles, War Diary, 6 June, 1944.

[173] Portugal, *We Were There,* 3033.

[174] Mark Zuehlke, *Holding Juno: Canada's Heroic Defence of D-Day Beaches: June 7-12,1944,* (Toronto: Douglas & McIntyre, 2006), 68-69.

[175] LAC, RG 24, Vol. 15,233, Royal Winnipeg Rifles, War Diary, June 1944, Appendix 6.

[176] LAC, RG 24, Vol. 15,233, Royal Winnipeg Rifles, War Diary, 6 June, 1944.

[177] Stacey described the attacks on the 7th Brigade on 7 and 8 June as a series of violent local counter attacks. This demonstrates the tone that Stacey had with the Canadians during the initial D-Day battles but understating the importance of these counter attacks and the abilities of the brigade.

[178] LAC, RG 24, Vol. 15,233, Royal Winnipeg Rifles, War Diary, 7 June 1944. The War Diary also states that C Company arrived an hour and a half after the rest of the battalion reached in Putot. They advanced by the wrong route.

[179] Stacey, *The Victory Campaign,* 125.

[180] The Reginas had a much better position for defensive at Bretteville and Norrey than the Winnipegs at Putot.

[181] Bechthold, "Defending the Normandy Bridgehead," 367.

[182] After walking the Putot-en Bessin battlefield while on the Canadian Battlefields Foundation Tour in June 2014, I was able to see just how difficult the defence of Putot was. On a map, it looks like it would be easily defensible, however, when on the actual grounds you see areas that could provide cover did not provide enough and the fields of fire were obstructed.

[183] Milner, *Stopping the Panzers,* 219.

184 Bechthold, "Defending the Normandy Bridgehead," 371.

185 Zuehike, *Holding Juno*, 152.

186 Reid, *Named by the Enemy*, 173.

187 Milner, *Stopping the Panzers,* 219. Headquarters also had every reason to except the British 69th Brigade to be in Brouay to help them if needed. They did not know that the British had been held up and would not be there to fill in the flank.

188 Portugal, *We Were There,* 2918.

189 Portugal, *We Were There,* 2918.

190 LAC, RG 24, Vol. 15,233, Royal Winnipeg Rifles, War diary, 7 June 1944.

191 Zuehike, *Holding Juno*, 161.

192 LAC, RG 24, Vol. 15,233, Royal Winnipeg Rifles, War Diary, June 1944, Appendix 6, Reid, 172.

193 Stacey, *The Victory Campaign*, 135.

194 Margolian, *Conduct Unbecoming*, 79.

195 Milner disagrees with that the number of tanks. However, he argues that there was a constant fear of panzers; therefore, easily leading itself to the exaggeration of the number of tanks involved in the battle. Milner, *Stopping the Panzers,* 245.

196 Milner, *Stopping the Panzers,* 245.

197 Ibid. 245.

198 Reid, *Named by the Enemy*, 172.

199 Portugal, *We Were There,* 3034.

200 Stacey, *The Victory Campaign*, 135.

201 LAC, RG 24, Vol. 15,233, Royal Winnipeg Rifles, War diary,8 June 1944.

202 Bechthold, "Defending the Normandy Bridgehead," 373.

203 LAC, RG 24, Vol. 15,233, Royal Winnipeg Rifles, War Diary, June 1944, Appendix 6.

204 Portugal, *We Were There*, 3067.

205 Margolian, *Conduct Unbecoming*, p. 16.

206 Portugal, *We Were There*, 2919-2920.

207 Tascona, Wells, *The Little Black Devils*, 152.

208 Milner, *Stopping the Panzers,* 247.

209 Portugal, *We Were There*, 3055.

210 Ibid. 3059.

211 LAC, RG 24, Vol. 15,233, Royal Winnipeg Rifles, War Diary, 8 June 1944.

212 Portugal, *We Were There,* 3044-3045, Reid, 173.

213 LAC, RG 24, Vol. 15,233, Royal Winnipeg Rifles, War Diary, 8 June 1944.

214 LAC, RG 24, Vol. 15,233, Royal Winnipeg Rifles, War Diary, June 1944, Appendix 6.

215 Bechthold, "Defending the Normandy Bridgehead," 376.

216 Reid, *Named by the Enemy*, 174.

217 Bechthold, "Defending the Normandy Bridgehead," 380.

218 Bechthold, "Defending the Normandy Bridgehead," 382.

219 Ibid. 382.

220 Margolian, *Conduct Unbecoming*, p. 80.

221 Inman, "'Hugs…Tears' As NB Veteran Relives D-Day," 12.

222 Stacey, *The Victory Campaign*, 118.

223 Copp, *Fields of Fire*, 13.

224 Stacey, *The Victory Campaign*, 136.

225 Brigadier H. F. Foster, "The Techniques of the Assault: The Canadian Army on D-Day, After-action reports by commanders," *Canadian Military History* 14.3 (Summer, 2005) 60.

226 English, *The Canadian Army*, 233n.

[227] Milner, *Stopping the Panzers*, 236.

[228] Zuehike, *Holding Juno,* 153.

[229] Bechthold, "Defending the Normandy Bridgehead," 367.

[230] Ibid. 376.

[231] Reid, *Named by the Enemy*, 175.

[232] S.P. MacKenzie, "The Treatment of Prisoners of War in World War II," *The Journal of Modern History* 66.3 (Sept. 1994), 487. This figure is far from exact because many countries did not keep proper records or they were unavailable to consult.

[233] Ibid. 487.

[234] Dominion of Canada, *International Convention Relative to the Treatment of Prisoners of War*, (Ottawa: F.A. Acland, King's Printer, 1935), 8

[235] Ibid, 8.

[236] The Japanese treated their POWs inhumanly. Memoirs from soldiers who survived their time in the Japanese POWs camps describe the conditions, diseases, work, and inhuman punishments that were inflicted upon them.

[237] Germany treated their POWs depending on their race and nationality. British, Canadian, and American POWs were treated significantly better than the Russian troops and Eastern Europeans. The Western Allies were originally treated well; however, as the war progressed the treatment deteriorated.

[238] MacKenzie, "The Treatment of Prisoner of War in World War II," 504.

[239] Ibid. 512.

[240] Ibid 514.

[241] A. Hamish Ion, "'Much Ado About Too Few': Aspects of the Treatment of Canadian and Commonwealth POWs and Civilian Internees in Metropolitan Japan, *Defense Studies* 6.3 (Sept. 2006), 296.

242 J. L. Granatstein, *Canada's Army: Waging War and Keeping the Peace*, (Toronto: University of Toronto Press, 2002), 196.

243 Many Canadians in Britain were disappointed that they were not chosen for this task since they had been overseas training. Instead, two units from Canada were dispatched.

244 Granatstein, *Canada's Army*, 199. The Japanese had no legal obligation in international law to follow the Geneva Convention.

245 Wyse took a great risk keeping this diary as the Japanese did not want them writing their experiences. That did not dissuade him from keeping the diary. It helped occupied the years in captivity. Many men decided to keep diaries of their experiences. Some had to go back to the camps after they were liberated to retrieve their writings.

246 Robert Wyse, *Bamboo Cage: The POW Diary of Flight Lieutenant Robert Wyse, 1942-1943*, Ed. Jonathan F. Vance (Fredericton, Goose Lane Editions, 2009), 17.

247 MacKenzie, "The Treatment of Prisoner of War in World War II," 515-516.

248 Dysentery was not like ordinary diarrhea, it was characterized by severe abdominal pain and frequent evacuation of stools containing blood lose and mucus. For most men the blood lose was considerable. Roland, *Long Night's Journey into Day*, 172.

249 Wyse, *Bamboo Cages*, 76.

250 Beriberi was caused by a prolonged deficiency in the diet of thiamine or vitamin B1. Pellagra is a disease of dermatitis, diarrhea, and dementia caused by the deficiency in niacin or nicotinic acid (vitamin B3). Electric feet was when the toes became numb, started twitching and would send shooting pains through the foot. It was believed that electric feet was a symptom of Beriberi. Roland, *Long Night's Journey into Day*, 139-140, 143, 151-152.

251 MacKenzie, "The Treatment of Prisoners of War in World War II," 514.

252 Roland, *Long Night's Journey into Day*, 93.

[253] Wyse, *Bamboo Cages*, 25. The POWs were not supposed to do any work that would help the enemy's operations of war.

[254] Roland, *Long Night's Journey into Day*, 94-95.

[255] The Geneva Convention dictated the penal laws that were used in the camps. The Japanese ignored these penal laws and took action into their own hands. Roland, *Long Night's Journey into Day*, 110.

[256] MacKenzie, "The Treatment of Prisoner of War in World War II," 515.

[257] Squad. Leader L. J. Birchall, 22 December 1943, LAC, Leonard Joseph Birchall fonds, R14039-0-1-E.

[258] Roland, *Long Night's Journey into Day*, 120.

[259] Nathan M. Greenfield, *The Damned: The Canadians at the Battle of Hong Kong and the POW Experience, 1941-1945*, 268.

[260] Wyse, *Bamboo Cages*, 52-53.

[261] The Chinese had the easiest time escaping and not getting recaptured because of their nationality.

[262] Wyse, *Bamboo Cages*, 86.

[263] Ibid. 85.

[264] The Japanese gave the prisoners a detailed list of how the postcards should be written. They had to be written in Japanese or English. No military information to be mentioned. They had to be written in black ink, in block letters, and only one line in each space. Letters had similar rules with a few added on including that the letters could only be two pages long and that they could not ask for food, medicine, or clothing. Birchall, 23 February 1944, LAC, Leonard Joseph Birchall fonds.

[265] L. J. Birchall to Mrs. Birchall, 9 December 1943, LAC, Leonard Joseph Birchall fonds.

[266] E. V. Danforth to Mrs. Birchall, 29 July 1944, Leonard Joseph Birchall fonds, LAC.

[267] Jack A Poolton, *Destined to Survive: A Dieppe Veteran's Story*, (Toronto: Dundurn Press, 1998), 41.

[268] The Germans were reported on killing severely wounded soldiers on the beaches. Poolton, *Destined to Survive*, 43.

[269] Ibid. 50.

[270] Poolton planned to go to Spain after escape or get in touch with the French underground, Ibid. 50.

[271] Ibid. 52.

[272] Some Normandy POWs were eventually placed in this camp.

[273] Poolton described his first experiences in the camp. He had to eat his soup from his boot while many others used rusty tin cans they had found in the garbage, Poolton, *Destined to Survive*, 56. John Mellor, *Forgotten Heroes: The Canadians at Dieppe,* (Toronto: Methuen, 1975), 105.

[274] The Red Cross had problems trying to inspect Japanese camps and send relief supplies because of the suspicion and obstructive attitude of the War Ministry. MacKenzie, "The Treatment of Prisoners of War in World War II," 515. This was a direct contrast to the Germans. They welcomed the relief supplies and often used the Red Cross inspections as propaganda films.

[275] Robert Prouse, *Ticket to Hell via Dieppe*, (Toronto: Van Nostrand Reinhold, 1982), 44.

[276] Vance, *Objects of Concern*, 147

[277] Jonathan F Vance, "Men in Manacles: The Shackling of Prisoners of War, 1942-1943," *Society for Military History* 59.3 (July 1995), 485.

[278] Stacey, *Six Years War*, 396.

[279] Prouse, *Ticket to Hell via Dieppe*, 35.

[280] Vance, "Men in Manacles," 486.

[281] Ibid. 485.

[282] Ibid. 486.

[283] Vance, "Men in Manacles," 496.

284 Jonathan F Vance, "The War Behind the Wire: The Battle to Escape from a German Prison Camp," *Journal of Contemporary History* 28.4 (Oct. 1993), 676.

285 Vance, "The War Behind the Wire: The Battle to Escape from a German Prison Camp," 688.

286 Poolton, *Destined to Survive*, 81.

287 Vance, *Objects of Concern*, 157.

288 Prouse, *Ticket to Hell via Dieppe*, 99.

289 Ibid. 100.

290 Mellor, *The Forgotten Heroes*, 139.

291 Margolian, *Conduct Unbecoming*, 80.

292 Margolian, *Conduct Unbecoming*, 81.

293 Margolian, *Conduct Unbecoming*, 82.

294 This was a direct violation of the Geneva Convention as soldiers were suppose to keep all personal effects in their possession. Dominion of Canada, 8.

295 Margolian, *Conduct Unbecoming*, 84.

296 Ibid. 87. There were no eye witnesses of these murders. Margolian uses forensic evidence and the accounts of two men who passed by the area before the murders took place to reconstruct the murders of the men from 9 Platoon. The Meakin brothers are buried in the Beny-sur-Mer cemetery. They are one of the nine sets of brothers who are buried there.

297 Barris, *Juno*, 111.

298 Portugal, *We Were There*, 3046. These murders are prime examples of how the Geneva Convention was tossed aside during the war. The SS Division did not follow the rules of war as other units did.

299 Portugal, *We Were There*, 3046.

300 Many of the 9th Brigade men who were taken prisoner during that battle never made it the German headquarters. They had been shot on the spot of capture or shot while being escorted to headquarters. Ian

Campbell, *Murder at the Abbaye: The Story of Twenty Canadian Soldiers Murder at the Abbaye d'Ardenne*, (Ottawa, The Golden Dog Press, 1996), 105.

[301] Margolian's *Conduct Unbecoming*, 68.

[302] Ibid. 69.

[303] Ibid. 70. No one saw these murders take place except for those who did the murdering. Margolian has pieced this together from the forensic evidence and hearsay witness testimony.

[304] Milner, *Stopping the Panzers*, 184. For a more detailed account of the murders by Meyer see Howard Margolian's *Conduct Unbecoming: The Story of the Murder of Canadian Prisoners of War in Normandy* or Ian Campbell's *Murder at the Abbaye: The Story of Twenty Canadian Soldiers Murder at the Abbaye d'Ardenne*.

[305] Margolian's *Conduct Unbecoming*, 74.

[306] After the Battle of Authie, 37 Canadians were murdered in the streets of the town trying to surrender to the Germans. The 12th SS took two of the Canadians and threw their bodies in the streets and ran over them with a tank until there was nothing left of their bodies, Margolian, p. 60.

[307] Ibid. 187.

[308] Fairweather was told by a German soldier that the Germans were not going to show mercy because of the Canadian bombing of Germany. Will R. Bird, *The Two Jacks*, 21.

[309] Inman, "'Hugs…Tears' As NB Veteran Relives D-Day," 12.

[310] Portugal, *We Were There*, 3059.

[311] Cavell always spoke of his dislike for turnips and his refusal to eat them.

[312] Learment recalled that their group was joined by another group of roughly 150 prisoners from various units including the majority coming from the Royal Winnipeg Rifles. Carvell could have been in this group that joined with Learment, Veness, and Fairweather; however, Carvell never made mention of this. Don Learment, "Soldier; POW,

Partisan: My Experience during the Battle of France, June-September 1944," *Canadian Military History* 9.2 (2000), 96-97.

313 Bird, *The Two Jacks*, 27.

314 George Carvell, War Claims Commission Form, 19 March 1954, Author's personal collection.

315 Bird, *The Two Jacks*, 30-32.

316 Learment, "Soldier; POW, Partisan," 97.

317 Bird, *The Two Jacks*, 25. Vance discusses that in 1942, officers took a course on how to avoid being captured, proper conduct in captivity, and equipment and techniques for escape. This course was only given once and only to officers, other ranks were not instructed in this material. It was not until after the Normandy invasion and the murders of the POWs from the 12th SS Panzer Division that the army began paying more attention to preparing soldiers for the possibility of captured. Vance, *Objects of Concern*, 101-102.

318 Bird, *The Two Jacks*, 42. Carvell would have marched a similar amount of miles; however, his group took longer to get to the camp than Veness and Fairweather.

319 Bird, *The Two Jacks*, 119.

320 Learment, "Soldier; POW, Partisan," 97.

321 Director of Records to Mrs. WM Carvell, Telegram, 25 June 1944, Author's personal collection.

322 At the beginning of the war, letters sent home from Britain usually took up to a month to arrive home. With Carvell being a POW, the letters would have been sent through the Red Cross back to Canada. There were many delays due to the war and the availability of planes to bring the mail over. Stacey and Wilson, *The Half Million*, 119.

323 The Germans had learned the numerous different ways to escape from the Dieppe POWs and how to prevent these escapes from occurring from the camps. These preventive tactics did not always ensure that escapes would not happen.

324 Bird, *The Two Jacks*, 43.

325 Bird, *The Two Jacks*, 44-45.

326 Bird, *The Two Jacks*, 44.

327 Inman, "'Hugs...Tears' As NB Veteran Relives D-Day, 12.

328 Unless otherwise indicated, specific information and stories related to Carvell are from the author's memory and from family members.

329 Bird, *The Two Jacks*, 45.

330 Some of the French girls would come by the fences, trying to give information to the prisoners until the Germans scared them away. Another French lady close to the camp would put her radio in the window, loud enough so the camp could hear the news. She did this until the Germans took her radio.

331 Bird, *The Two Jacks*, 51.

332 Learment, "Soldier; POW, Partisan," 98.

333 Carvell, War Claims Commission Form, 19 March 1954, Author's personal collection.

334 Bird, *The Two Jacks*, 54.

335 Carvell, War Claims Commission Form, 19 March 1954, Author's personal collection.

336 The men would chew slowly, trying to savour every bite of the food and try to restrict themselves from eating all the food at once.

337 Bird, *The Two Jacks*, 74.

338 Learment, "Soldier; POW, Partisan," 99.

339 Portugal, *We Were There*, 3060.

340 George Carvell to Mrs. WM Carvell, September 1944, Author's personal collection.

341 Inman, "'Hugs...Tears' As NB Veteran Relives D-Day", 12.

342 Samuel Fuller, *A Third Face - My Tale of Writing, Fighting, and Filmmaking*, ebook edition, 2002.

343 George Carvell to Mrs. WM Carvell, 7 December 1944, Author's personal collection.

344 George Carvell to Mrs. WM Carvell, January 1945, Author's personal collection.

345 Many men took the necessities to help them survive the journey, while others tried to take some souvenirs with them. Poolton originally decided to take a set of the chains that were used during the shackling; however, he realized, during the march, that they were just too heavy to continue carrying them. Poolton, *Destined to Survive*, 103.

346 Poolton, *Destined to Survive*, 104.

347 Poolton, *Destined to Survive*, 104.

348 Poolton recalls how a foreign soldier had stole from another and the Germans had to place him in another area because they men were going to kill him for stealing. Poolton protected the man from his group of people. Ibid. 111-112.

349 Poolton, *Destined to Survive*, 106.

350 John Freund, *Spring's End*, Toronto: The Azrieli Foundation, 2007, 65.

351 Martin Gilbert, *The Holocaust: The Jewish Tragedy*, London: Fontana Press, 1987, 776.

352 Ibid. 789.

353 Inman, "'Hugs…Tears' As NB Veteran Relives D-Day", 12.

354 Ibid.

355 Carvell, War Claims Commission Form, 19 March 1954, Author's personal collection.

356 Inman, "'Hugs…Tears' As NB Veteran Relives D-Day", 12.

357 The actual date of liberation is questioned. Some sources say 6 May, others 9 May.

358 Marsha Orgeron, "Liberating Images? Samuel Fuller's Film of Falkeneu Concentration Camp," *Film Quarterly* 60.2 (2006), 46n.

359 Fuller, *A Third Face*.

360 Fuller, *A Third Face.*

361 Fuller used the images he captured in his semi-autographical film *The Big Red One*(1980). They were used in Emil Weiss' documentary *Falkenau: The Impossible*(1988) and Fuller discusses the Falkenau footage in detail. Both of these films can be found on the internet.

362 Orgeron, 39.

363 George Carvell, Medical History of an Invalid, 17 May 1945, Author's personal collection.

364 Carvell, War Claims Commission Form, 19 March 1954, Author's personal collection.

365 Tim Cook, *Fight to the Finish*, 404.

366 Cook, *Fight to the Finish*, 406, J. L. Granatstein, *The Best Little Army in the World*, 252.

367 Cook, *Fight to the Finish*, 412

368 Cook, *Fight to the Finish*, 406.

369 Cook, *Fight to the Finish,* 416.

370 Ibid.

371 Cook, 417.

372 Carvell's service file, Training Employment - Department of Veterans Affairs, 28 August 1945, Author's personal collection.

373 Inman, "'Hugs...Tears' As NB Veteran Relives D-Day," 12.

374 Copp and McAndrew, *Battle Exhaustion.* 152.

375 Tim Cook, *Shock Troops: Canadians Fighting the Great War, 1917-1918*, 242.

376 Ibid. 243.

377 Coop and McAndrew, *Battle Exhaustion*, 153.

378 Cook, *Fight to the Finish*, 236.

379 Ibid, 423.

[380] Carvell's service file, Author's personal collection.

[381] Directorate of History and Heritage (DHH), Historical Report: The Carleton & York Regiment, 1948-1952.

[382] Carvell's service file, Author's personal collection.

[383] Inman, "'Hugs...Tears' As NB Veteran Relives D-Day," 12.

[384] Corinne Fizherbert, "Written in Stone," *The Daily Gleaner*, 5 October 2010.

[385] For more information about the Canadian Battlefields Foundation see http://www.cbf-fccb.ca/.

[386] C.P. Stacey and John English are critical of the quality of the Canadian Army training. Mark Zuehlke and Jonathan Vance are more critical of the training the reinforcement units and there preparedness for battle.

[387] Colonel C.P. Stacey, *Official History of the Canadian Army in the Second World War, Vol 1: Six Years of War: The Army in Canada, Britain and the Pacific*, (Ottawa: Queen's Printer and Controller of Stationery, 1955), 133.

[388] Stacey, *Six Years of War*, 243.

[389] Stacey, *Six Years of War*, 253.

[390] Colonel C.P. Stacey, *Official History of the Canadian Army in the Second World War, Vol II1 The Victory Campaign: The Operations in North-West Europe, 1944-1945*, (Ottawa: Queen's Printer and Controller of Stationery, 1960), 35-36.

[391] Ibid.

[392] John A English, *The Canadian Army and the Normandy Campaign: A Study of Failure in High Command*, New York: Praeger, 1991, xiv.

[393] Ibid. 110.

[394] English, *The Canadian Army and the Normandy Campaign*, 152.

[395] English, *The Canadian Army and the Normandy Campaign*, 144-145.

[396] Ibid. p. 306.

[397] Ibid. 312. Stacey also believed that the Germans were of superior strength and skill than that of the Canadians.

[398] Captain Harold Macdonald with M.A. MacDonald, "The Long Wait (Part 1): A Personal Account of Infantry Training in Britain, June 1942-June 1943," *Canadian Military History* 15.2, (Spring 2006), p. 40.

[399] Ibid. 46.

[400] Stacey, *The Victory Campaign*, 118.

[401] Ibid. 135.

[402] Ibid. 136.

[403] Marc Milner, *Stopping the Panzers: The Untold Story of D-Day*, (Lawrence, Kansas: University Press of Kansas, 2014), 9. Stacey and his staff did not have access to all the necessary documents needed for writing the history even though they were the official historians of the war. This impacted how the history was told.

[404] Milner, *Stopping the Panzers*, 15.

[405] Stacey, *The Victory Campaign*, 271.

[406] Ibid. 274.

[407] While Stacey is highly critical of the regimental officers, English argues that it was the higher command of the Canadian army that failed. The higher command failed to train their officers properly which led to their troops not being trained properly.

[408] Stacey, *The Victory Campaign*, 275.

[409] Terry Copp, *Fields of Fire: The Canadians in Normandy*, (Toronto: University of Toronto Press, 2003), 13.

[410] Copp, *Fields of Fire*, 260.

[411] This approach of reconstructing the invasion from these sources is different from the top down approach that Stacey used for his official histories.

[412] Copp, *Fields of Fire*, 57.

413 Stacey has a chapter concluding his discussion of Normandy called "Normandy: A Balance Sheet." Copp uses this title to portray the new version of this history.

414 Copp, *Fields of Fire,* 255.

415 Milner, *Stopping the Panzers*, 7.

416 Milner, *Stopping the Panzers*, 219.

417 Ibid. 315.

418 Reid, *Named by the Enemy*, 175.

419 Ted Barris, *Juno: Canadians at D-Day, June 6, 1944*, (Toronto: Thomas Allen Publishers, 2004), 7.

420 Barris, *Juno*, 111.

421 Mike Bechthold, "Defending the Normandy Bridgehead: The Battles for Putot-en-Bessin, 7-9 June 1944," in *Canada and the Second World War: Essays in Honour of Terry* Copp, eds. Geoffrey Hayes, Mike Bechthold, and Matt Symes, (Waterloo: Wilfred Laurier Press, 2012), 376.

422 English, 233n.

423 Bechthold, "Defending the Normandy Bridgehead," 376.

424 Bechthold, "Defending the Normandy Bridgehead," 378.

425 Fifty of the prisoners were executed by the 12th SS Panzer Division.

426 This again argues against English's belief that the Canadian command led to the Canadian failure. This also argues against Stacey's belief that the Canadians had a lack of tactical skill.

427 Daniel G. Dancocks, *In Enemy Hands: Canadian Prisoners of War, 1939-45*, (Edmonton: Hurtig Publishers, 1983), ix.

428 Dancocks, *In Enemy Hands,* 152.

429 Jonathan Vance, *Objects of Concern: Canadian Prisoners of War Through the Twentieth Century*, (Vancouver: UBC Press, 1994), 251.

430 Ibid. 100.

431 Vance, *Objects of Concern,* 217.

432 Ibid. 223.

433 Howard Margolian, *Conduct Unbecoming: The Story of the Murder of Canadian Prisoners of War in Normandy*, (Toronto: University of Toronto Press, 1998), ix. The book was the first to capture this dark moment in detail. Recent scholarship has added to the literature on this topic.

434 Margolian, *Conduct Unbecoming*, 187.

435 See Margolian, *Conduct Unbecoming*, 86-87 for the reconstruction of 13 deaths from the Winniepgs in the final group.

436 Veness and Fairweather were placed in a barn in the Abbeye while Myer's men were killing the Canadian prisoners in the garden. Will R Bird, *The Two Jacks: The Amazing Adventures of Major Jack M. Veness and Major Jack L. Fairweather*, (Philadelphia, Macrae Smith, 1955), 21.

437 Carvell's only letter from this camp appears to be scripted. Veness wrote the same letter home when he arrived at the camp. Bird, *The Two Jacks*, 119.

438 J. L. Granatstein, *Canada's Army: Waging War and Keeping the Peace*, (Toronto: University of Toronto Press, 2002), 196.

439 Many Canadians in Britain were disappointed that they were not chosen for this task since they had been overseas training. Instead, two units from Canada were dispatched.

440 Granatstein, *Canada's Army*, 199. The Japanese had no legal obligation in international law to follow the Geneva Convention.

441 Charles G. Roland, *Long Night's Journey into Day: Prisoners of War in Hong Kong and Japan, 1941-1945*, (Waterloo, Wilfred Laurier University Press, 2001), xiii.

442 Sending and receiving mail was very limited. When prisoners were allowed to write home it was censored and only a few lines long.

443 Roland, *Long Night's Journey into Day*, 91.

444 Jack Poolton, *Destined to Survive: A Dieppe Veteran's Story*, (Toronto: Dundurn Press, 1998), 41.

[445] The Germans did this in retaliation for the belief that the Allies bound the hands of German POWs in Dieppe.

[446] A. Robert Prouse, *Ticket to Hell via Dieppe*, (Toronto, Van Nostrand Reinhold, 1982), 99.

[447] Terry Copp and Bill McAndrew, *Battle Exhaustion: Soldiers and Psychiatrists in the Canadian Army, 1939-1945,* (Montreal: McGill-Queen's University Press, 1990), 4.

[448] Ibid. 4.

[449] Copp and McAndrew, *Battle Exhaustion*. 152.

[450] Ibid. 153.

BIBLIOGRAPHY

Archives

Directorate of History and Heritage, National Defence HQ, Ottawa, Ontario

Library and Archives Canada, Ottawa Ontario

Published and Other Sources

Barris, Ted. *Juno: Canadians at D-Day, June 6, 1944.* Toronto: Thomas Allen Publishers, 2004.

Bechthold, Mike. "Defending the Normandy Bridgehead: The Battles for Putot-en-Bessin, 7-9 June 1944," in *Canada and the Second World War: Essays in Honour of Terry* Copp, eds. Geoffrey Hayes, Mike Bechthold, and Matt Symes. 367-389. Waterloo: Wilfred Laurier Press, 2012.

Bird, Will R. *The Two Jacks: The Amazing Adventures of Major Jack M. Veness and Major Jack L. Fairweather.* Philadelphia, Macrae Smith, 1955.

Campbell, Ian. *Murder at the Abbaye: The Story of Twenty Canadian Soldiers Murder at the Abbaye d'Ardenne.* Ottawa, The Golden Dog Press, 1996.

Cook, Tim. *Shock Troops: Canadians Fighting the Great War, 1917-1918, Vol. 2.* Toronto: Penguin Group, 2008.

_____. *The Necessary War: Canadians Fighting the Second World War, 1939-1943, Vol.1.* Toronto: Penguin Group, 2014.

_____. *Fight to the Finish: Canadians Fighting the Second World War, 1944-1945, Vol.2.* Toronto: Penguin Group, 2015.

Copp, Terry. *Fields of Fire: The Canadians in Normandy.* Toronto: University of Toronto Press, 2003.

Copp, Terry and Bill McAndrew. *Battle Exhaustion: Soldiers and Psychiatrists in the Canadian Army, 1939-1945.* Montreal: McGill-Queen's University Press, 1990.

Dancocks, Daniel G. *In Enemy Hands: Canadian Prisoners of War, 1939-45.* Edmonton: Hurtig Publishers, 1983.

Dominion of Canada. *International Convention Relative to the Treatment of Prisoners of War.* Ottawa: F.A. Acland, King's Printer, 1935.

English, John A. *The Canadian Army and the Normandy Campaign: A Study of Failure in High Command.* New York: Praeger, 1991.

Fizherbert, Corinne. "Written in Stone," *The Daily Gleaner*, 5 October 2010.

Fobes, E.R. "The 1930s: The Depression and Retrenchment," E.R. Fobes eds. *The Atlantic Provinces in Confederation.* 272-305. Toronto: University of Toronto Press, 1993

Foster, Brigadier H. F. "The Techniques of the Assault: The Canadian Army on D-Day, After-action reports by commanders." *Canadian Military History* 14, no. 3 (Summer, 2005):

Freund, John. *Spring's End.* Toronto: The Azrieli Foundation, 2007.

Gilbert, Martin. *The Holocaust: The Jewish Tragedy.* London: Fontana Press, 1987.

Graham, Howard. *Citizen and Soldier: The Memoirs of Lieutenant General Howard Graham.* Toronto: McClelland and Stewart, 1987.

Granatstein, J. L. *Canada's Army: Waging War and Keeping the Peace.* Toronto: University of Toronto Press, 2002.

_____. *Best Little Army in the World: The Canadians in Northwest Europe, 1944-1945.* Toronto: HarperCollins Canada, 2015.

Greenfield, Nathan M. *The Damned: The Canadians at the Battle of Hong Kong and the POW Experience, 1941-1945.* Toronto: HarperCollins Canada, 2010.

Historical Section of the General Staff. *The Canadian in Britain, 1939-44.* Ottawa: The King's Printer, 1944.

Ion, A. Hamish. "'Much Ado About Too Few': Aspects of the Treatment of Canadian and Commonwealth POWs and Civilian Internees in Metropolitan Japan." *Defense Studies* 6, no. 3 (Sept. 2006): 292-317.

Inman, Monica. "'Hugs...Tears' As NB Veteran Relives D-Day," *The Victory County Record*, 10 November 1994, 12

Learment, Don. "Soldier; POW, Partisan: My Experience during the Battle of France, June-September 1944," *Canadian Military History* 9, no. 2 (2000): 91-104.

Macdonald, Captain Harold, with M.A. MacDonald, "The Long Wait (Part 1): A Personal Account of Infantry Training in Britain, June 1942-June 1943," *Canadian Military History* 15, no. 2, (Spring 2006): 35-50.

MacKenzie, S.P. "The Treatment of Prisoners of War in World War II," *The Journal of Modern History* 66, no. 3, (Sept. 1994): 487-520.

Maclay, Mark. *Aldershot's Canadians: In Love and War 1939-45.* Farnborough, Applin, 1997.

Margolian, Howard. *Conduct Unbecoming: The Story of the Murder of Canadian Prisoners of War in Normandy.* Toronto: University of Toronto Press, 1998.

Mellor, John. *Forgotten Heroes: The Canadians at Dieppe.* Toronto: Methuen, 1975.

Milner, Marc. *Stopping the Panzers: The Untold Story of D-Day.* Lawrence, Kansas: University Press of Kansas, 2014.

Mowat, Farley. *And No Bird Sang.* Toronto: McClelland and Stewart, 1979.

Orgeron, Marsha. "Liberating Images? Samuel Fuller's Film of Falkeneu Concentration Camp," *Film Quarterly* 60, no. 2 (2006): 38-47.

Poolton, Jack. *Destined to Survive: A Dieppe Veteran's Story*. Toronto: Dundurn Press, 1998.

Portugal, Jean E. *We Were There: The Army, A Record for Canada*, vol. 6. Toronto: Royal Canadian Military Institute Heritage Society, 1998.

Prouse, A. Robert. *Ticket to Hell via Dieppe*. Toronto, Van Nostrand Reinhold, 1982.

Reid, Brian. *Named by the Enemy: A History of the Royal Winnipeg Rifles*. Altona, Manitoba: Robin Brass Studio, Inc, 2010.

Ripley, Donald. *The Home Front: Wartime Life in Camp Aldershot and Kentville, Nova Scotia*. Hantsport: Lancelot Press, 1992.

Roland, Charles G. *Long Night's Journey into Day: Prisoners of War in Hong Kong and Japan, 1941-1945*. Waterloo, Wilfred Laurier University Press, 2001.

Stacey, Colonel C.P. *The Canadian Army 1939-1945*. Ottawa: King's Printer, 1948.

_____.*Official History of the Canadian Army in the Second World War, Vol 1: Six Years of War: The Army in Canada, Britain and the Pacific*. Ottawa: Queen's Printer and Controller of Stationery, 1955.

_____.*Official History of the Canadian Army in the Second World War, Vol II1 The Victory Campaign: The Operations in North-West Europe, 1944-1945*. Ottawa: Queen's Printer and Controller of Stationery, 1960.

Stacey C.P. and Barbara M. Wilson. *The Half Million: The Canadians in Britain, 1939-1946*. Toronto: University of Toronto Press, 1987.

Tascna, Bruce and Eric Wells. *The Little Black Devils: A History of the Royal Winnipeg Rifles*. Manitoba: Frye Publishing, 1983.

Vance, Jonathan F. "The War Behind the Wire: The Battle to Escape from a German Prison Camp," *Journal of Contemporary History* 28, no. 4 (Oct. 1993): 675-693.

_____.*Objects of Concern: Canadian Prisoners of War Through the Twentieth Century.* Vancouver: UBC Press, 1994.

_____. "Men in Manacles: The Shackling of Prisoners of War, 1942-1943," *Society for Military History* 59, no. 3 (July 1995): 483-504.

_____. "Captured in the Victory Campaign: Surrenders of Canadian Troops in North-West Europe, 1944-1945," in *World War II: Variants and Visions*, ed., Thomas O. Kelly II. Collingdale, PA: Diane Publishing, 1999: 125-144.

_____.*Maple Leaf Empire: Canada, Britain, and Two World Wars.* Toronto: OUP Canada, 2012.

Wyse, Robert. *Bamboo Cage: The POW Diary of Flight Lieutenant Robert Wyse, 1942-1943*, Ed. Jonathan F. Vance. Fredericton, Goose Lane Editions, 2009.

Zuehike, Mark. *Holding Juno: Canada's Heroic Defence of D-Day Beaches: June 7-12,1944.* Toronto: Douglas & McIntyre, 2006.

About Lammi Publishing, Inc.

Incorporated in 2014, Lammi Publishing is dedicated to publishing Canadian military history from the wars before confederation to the mission in Afghanistan. Our philosophy is that we cannot forget. Our mission is to be a method of remembrance. Canadian military history has shaped not only our politics and government, but our society as well. Canadians naturally take pride in our famous victories in Western Europe, Afghanistan and South Africa. From the oceans to the air, Canadians have done their duty with skill and valor. Peacekeeping operations have taken our forces far and wide bringing hope and security to so many. Canadian uniforms have been seen around the world as harbingers of liberation, from Belgium in WWI to the Netherlands in WWII to Yugoslavia in the 1990s.

It is only by having easy access to material on these events that we can understand them, put them in context and remember. Information, analysis, and the memoires of those who served should be readily available instead of being locked away in a desk or a long-forgotten bookcase in the back of a library.

The rise of electronic books means that it is now possible for anyone to easily compile a library that would rival the best that our public libraries or universities can offer, with no more worries about short print runs and the vagaries of the antiquarian market.

To learn more about us and what we are doing, check out our website.

http://lammipublishing.ca